We Can Get The

Finding personal deliverance through simple acts of spiritual war.

Bob!! @
Thank you for
playing my song —
I really appreciate
it.

By Lenny Ouradnik

Printed in the United States of America

First Printing, 2013

ISBN- 978-1493781362

Lenny Ouradnik

Coon Rapids MN 54433

763-757-6697

This book is dedicated to my fabulous Babe!

Donna, in a million years, I couldn't have done this without you!

Thank you

Table of Contents

Preface

I grew up in a Christian home, sort of. When I was born, neither of my parents were believers. Although my father had committed his life to Christ when he was a teenager, he was far from God until I was about six years old. That year, 1966, two of my father's relatives were killed in a car accident. While they were on the way to North Dakota for the funerals, two more of my father's relatives were killed in a second car accident. This, of course, was devastating to my father and he decided then to recommit his life to Jesus Christ. My mother, on the other hand, was very skeptical.

When I was about seven years old we moved to a suburb of Minneapolis, Minnesota. Shortly after our move, Fred and Char moved into our neighborhood with their children. This was in the day when everyone greeted new neighbors. My mother went to meet the new family and got to know them. It wasn't long until Fred led my mother to Jesus and then into baptism in the Holy Spirit and speaking in tongues. Shortly after that my dad was baptized in the Holy Spirit and he, too, spoke in tongues.

About three years later we made another move. This time we moved to a small town in northern Minnesota. Not long after we settled in my father started a Friday night fellowship that lasted several years. Through it, literally hundreds of college kids were led to Christ and into the baptism of the Holy Spirit.

At these meetings, we would occasionally see people exhibit manifestations of demonic influence. I remember one person who became stiff as a board during the worship time and then let out a shriek. When things like this happened, these folks were led down to the basement of the house where we met. Several men from the fellowship would then pray for deliverance for these people by casting out demons and praying for them to be released from demonic oppression.

When this ministry time was completed, those that were prayed for would report that they felt released from problems they had never been able to overcome before. They said that they were finally able to feel God's love and know Him better than ever before.

The idea of this was so exciting to me that I started to read books about deliverance so that I would know more about it. Then I tried to do deliverance on my own. Sometimes when I was talking to my friends I'd listen to them talk about problems like those people I had seen during ministry times at the fellowship. They would tell me that they were afraid or angry; some of them said they felt life was hopeless. I'd pray for my friends like I had seen the elders and my father pray. If my friends were afraid I would try to cast out a spirit of fear. If they were having difficulties with their parents I would try to cast out a spirit of rejection. I know some of the prayers for my friends were successful, but looking back it's clear that I was very naïve about the whole thing.

About a year after the fellowship ended I left home and I fell away from the Lord. I fell away from the Lord mostly because I only had my parent's relationship with Christ, not my own. In other words, I lived a Christian life while I was a child in my parent's home, and when I left I didn't have my own foundation in Christ to stand on.

When I came back to the Lord I had a lot of difficulties in my life. I thought if I read the books about deliverance again I would learn how to solve some of my problems. Then I remembered the things that I observed during the Friday night fellowship, and I tried to deliver myself from my problems (What I tried to do is sometimes referred to as spiritual warfare. We'll use this term frequently in this book). I found that I was quite unsuccessful at improving my life.

Ultimately, this is what I discovered: All the knowledge I had from reading books and witnessing deliverance didn't bring change to my life. I felt quite humbled when I recognized that for all my reading and all my experience I couldn't even solve my own problems. It felt like I had a giant brain and a tiny, little spiritual body.

As a kid I would look at advertisements for books on bodybuilding by Charles Atlas. These ads had a picture of a skinny kid getting sand kicked in his face by a big muscle-bound bully. The kid was the "98-pound weakling." In my spirit at the time, I felt like I was that 98-pound weakling. Satan was the jerk kicking sand in my face and I didn't know what to do about it.

When I went to the Lord, took responsibility for my behavior and asked Him to help change me, I began to understand there was more to spiritual warfare than I knew. When I began to take responsibility for who I was and repented of my thoughts and actions, the Lord began to intervene in my life, producing everlasting change for the better.

How many of us are like that 98-pound weakling in our spiritual development? We don't have the strength or the know-how to stand up to that jerk kicking sand in our face. Most of us would be hard-pressed to name any spiritual weapon, let alone use one or more of them to gain victory over a difficult circumstance. Most of us are pretty immature in our walk with Christ. Sure, some of us have taken time to learn scriptures and study topics that are interesting to us; we could say that we are intellectually well developed. We may take time to exercise and stay in shape; we could say that we are physically well developed. We have done a pretty good job of making our brains very smart and our bodies strong. But we have forgotten that we need to teach our hearts. According to the Bible, our intellect, great though it may be, is as foolishness to God (1 Corinthians 3:19), and our bodies go from dust to dust (Genesis 3:19). Christ was certainly concerned about our bodies and brains. He did say that we should love God with all of our mind and all of our strength (Mark 12:30). He also said that we should love him with all of our soul and all of our heart.

How can we learn to love the Lord with all of our heart? In both the Hebrew and the Greek the "heart" refers to our innermost being. It is the place where we think, reflect, decide or choose; it is where we carry our morals and it is where our thoughts, passions, desires, appetites and affections sit (from Thayer and Smith. "Greek Lexicon entry for 'Kardia'". "The NAS New Testament Greek Lexicon". . 1999). There is no question whether we should use our brains to learn about God. We should. At the same time, it would be unwise to neglect the teaching of our hearts. Unfortunately, there has been little encouragement and even less instruction to help Christians learn the basic principles that will help them teach their hearts to be strong enough to overcome difficult circumstances.

Jesus said His yoke is easy and His burden is light (Matt. 11:30), so there must be a simple way to overcome our circumstances. How can we understand spiritual warfare at its most basic level? How can we conduct spiritual warfare regardless of our circumstance? Can we only find deliverance by visiting with some guru-like person who is at once fearsome and awesome because he or she seems to hear from God? How can we find personal deliverance using the simplest of weapons at our disposal?

What are the simplest weapons at our disposal? The simple weapons we're referring to are these: 1) choosing to become a thankful person; 2) establishing a personal worship connection with God; and 3) honoring and forgiving the people in your life.

When we come to a saving knowledge of Christ we are mostly left to discover the things of God and His kingdom on our own. The problem with this is that we easily bypass the actual process of growing in the Lord. We're not given any order for growth; we're not told what's important. Worse, even the things we know are important are hard, because no one is teaching us how to understand them, how to implement them in our lives. And these are the results:

- We don't know how to read the Bible and understand what it really tells us to do. **We are ignorant.**

- We don't know how to pray. Because we don't know how to pray our prayers are ineffective for the most part. **We are ineffective**.

- We don't know how to really fellowship and share our problems with anyone and tell them the truth about how things really are. We think if we were honest about our circumstances others would actually find out what wretches we are, and they would never want to be with us anymore. **We are afraid.**

Many of us in the church have been led to believe we have to be afraid of Satan and his army because they are so powerful. We've been led to believe that it is only the super-spiritual, super-mature person who can deal with the enemy with any success, and that we will be hurt very badly if we try to mess with him. We have been led to believe that Satan is like Goliath and we should always be afraid of him.

None of this is true. We forget that David was a rather small, very young man who stood up to Goliath and not only pushed him back, but slew him and cut his head off. Then he held Goliath's head up for all to see and made a show of his defeat.

This book will put weapons in your hands that you can wield regardless of how long you've been a believer, regardless of how dire your situation. And you will find that as you wield these weapons, practicing with them daily, your life will begin to change. These weapons are easy enough to use every day, even every minute if you have to. Use them in the battles that suffocate you and prevent you from living the life God has promised us as members of His family. This is our purpose. We will learn how to make choices that turn simple principles into spiritual weapons of war. The simple principles we're referring to are these: 1) choosing to become a thankful person; 2) establishing a personal worship connection with God; and 3) honoring and forgiving the people in your life.

We can get there from here. We can get to the place with God we've hungered and thirsted for. We can get to the place of freedom we've searched for. We can get to the place of peace that has eluded us. We will learn together how to teach our hearts to fight the battles the enemy brings to us. We will find our personal deliverance and we will find our way to a closer, more meaningful relationship with the Lord.

Chapter 1

Haven't We Been Here Before?

If there's an easy way to do something, I'll try to find it.

I spend a lot of energy looking for the easiest way to do something or the quickest way to get where I am going. I'm not sure, but I think I spend at least as much time taking care of the mistakes I make when I take these shortcuts as I do fixing the original problem. Like the time I tried to fix the toilet leak the easy way. I figured if I just turned the nut on the valve a little bit tighter the leak would go away. It turns out that porcelain is brittle.

After I cleaned up the mess and explained to my wife what happened, I made the trip to the building center to buy a new toilet. Then I made another trip to the hardware store for another part … and then another trip for yet another part to complete the job. A simple 15-minute job turned into an 8-hour job by the time I was done. Easy, right?

I've learned in my Christian walk that you have to take every single step of the journey. Taking a shortcut usually leads to the longer, harder path. Have you ever experienced a difficult time and it felt like you'd been there before? I know there have been times in my life when I felt like I was going through the same difficult experience over and over again. As we'll discuss later, until I was about 30 years old I had a hard time keeping jobs. I'd accept a job, have a great start, and then have trouble with my co-workers or my boss, and the next thing you know I was looking for another job. I began to believe I would never be able to keep a job. Have you ever been through a time like this? Everyone else seems to be doing just fine, but you're having all of this trouble, and it's not the first time?

Many of us have heard someone we know and trust talk about how they were healed or set free or how they found God's love. We think if we do what they did, the same thing will happen for us. But we forget what they went through to find that wonderful experience. We forget their pain and suffering. We forget their struggle to maintain their faith in God during a difficult time. We think if it worked for our friends it should work for us.

This idea leads us to believe we can jump ahead and skip the lessons we think are unimportant. I wish it were true. I sometimes think that we're a lot like pioneers who know the way to the West. We point to the West and say, "It's that way!" But knowing how to get somewhere isn't the same as making the journey.

When we approach our Christian walk by finding the easiest way to get from here to there, we can become disconnected from the reality of what it takes to get where we want to go. This approach to our walk is missing something.

Do you think you could simply read a book about how to surgically remove an appendix and then walk into an operating room to perform the surgery? No one in his or her right mind would think this is a good plan. Surgeons dedicate their lives to the practice of surgery. They have to work hard and excel in their education. They work and work and work. Becoming a surgeon requires years of education and practice.

It's the same for a believer who wants to walk with God. If we are to be excellent, mature Christians, we have to take *all* of the steps of the journey. To find our route we must study the map, which is the Bible, until we understand the direction we should go. It's good that we're not required to go on this journey alone. In fact, if we do, we're more likely to fail to reach our destination. We are advised to reach out for help from God and from others on the same journey. There are many with us on this journey that have learned how to understand the directions. They know what it takes to walk through the steps we are going through.

Many of us approach our walk with God from an intellectual, physical-world mindset. But our journey includes a need for faith and an understanding of the spiritual world. Our relationship with God requires a balanced blend of our brains and our hearts. We have knowledge of our salvation in our brains, but the meaning and depth of it is understood in our hearts. It takes time for our hearts to understand the meaning and depth of our salvation.

Our hearts have to be taught what we have learned in our brains. That's why it often takes us several times to come to the Lord. At first we only have an intellectual knowledge of what we have done. But after walking with the Lord for some time, that knowledge transfers to our hearts. Someone could hold a gun to our heads and demand that we recant, that we change our belief that Jesus is our Lord and Savior and we would say "to live is Christ, to die is gain" (Philippians 1:21).

We must understand just knowing what the principles are is not very useful in our Christian walk. I have a frying pan at home. I know what it is and that I can use it to cook eggs. But I had to learn how to use it. When I first started cooking eggs, I wasn't very good at it. I really like eggs and omelets so I continued to cook them until I became pretty good at it. Now I can whip up an omelet in my pan and it comes out perfect almost all the time. In the same way, we must become skillful in our use of these principles through continual practice.

We must teach our hearts the simple principles of walking with God. These principles are useful in our walk with God in three ways. First, learning and using them will help us grow in our relationship with God. Second, these ideas help us defend against the tactics of our enemy as he looks for ways to destroy our faith. Finally, we will have an offensive weapon to help us overcome our circumstances.

Over time you will see that learning and practicing these principles will reveal them to be great weapons in many of the spiritual battles you face very day. The simple principles we're referring to are these: 1) choosing to become a thankful person; 2) establishing a personal worship connection with God; and 3) honoring and forgiving the people in your life.

Learning these principles and understanding them as weapons will help us gain victory over our current circumstances in at least two ways. As we continue to grow in our use and practice of them, we'll find that we are able to fend off attacks and avoid being drawn into the battles that have crippled us in the past. Furthermore, the use and practice of these simple weapons of warfare will serve to ready us for the more mature, more advanced activities of warfare.

Practice is vital to the process of growth. The practice principle applies to every area of our lives whether we are student-athletes, administrative assistants, sales people or CEOs.

When a pro ball team begins to have troubles after some success, we almost always hear them talk about going "back to the basics." If it's baseball, they practice the double play. If it's basketball, they practice passing and free throws. If it's football, they go back to the playbook and run and rerun the routes or practice their blocks and tackles. If someone making millions of dollars per year to throw or catch a ball needs to go back to the basics when they experience difficulty with their game, how much more do those of us who stand to inherit uncountable riches need to do the same?

This book will focus on our prayer and thought lives and it will impact how we read and act on the scriptures. Where possible, we'll take the mystery out of the concept of spiritual warfare, and we will learn how to use the simplest weapons of spiritual warfare: Becoming a thankful person, establishing a worship connection with God and honoring the people in our lives.

To begin with, it's important we agree that we live in a spiritual world that is at war. To demonstrate this idea we can look to the Bible, other cultures and our own experience.

Let's review a few of the stories in the Bible and see how they refer to some kind of world beyond ours:

- Jacob wrestled with the Lord (Genesis 32:22-31).
- Balaam's donkey saw an angel and then spoke to Balaam (Numbers 22).
- Daniel saw an angel (Daniel 10)
- Enoch and Elijah were caught up by the Lord and never died (Genesis 5:24, 2 Kings 2:1-12).
- Elisha opened the eyes of his servant to see the angels standing with them against the big army (2 Kings 6:8-22).
- Ezekiel spoke to the dry bones (Ezekiel 37:1-13).
- Satan tempted Jesus and angels ministered to Him after the experience (Matthew 4:1-11).

- Jesus sent a legion of demons into a herd of pigs (Mark 5:1-18).
- Jesus rose from the dead (Matthew 28:1-8, Mark 16:1-8, Luke 24:1-12, John 20:1-8).

It's interesting that every culture in the world recognizes a spiritual world. We make fun of it sometimes, looking down on cultures and tribes that believe in witch doctors and casting spells and curses. In spite of our maltreatment of these cultural beliefs, they remain consistent throughout the world. Many of these cultures believe that the spiritual world is more "real" than the physical world. (See Boyd: God At War, pp 11-14, 1997 Intervarsity Press).

Maybe when you were a child you went camping with some friends and told ghost stories. You might have had a déjà vu experience. Are you afraid of things that go bump in the night? Have you ever looked up your horoscope or had your palm read? These are examples of our fascination with the spiritual world. Even though we can't scientifically prove that there is a spiritual world existing all around us, many people believe that there is.

When Satan deceived Adam and Eve, they allowed him access to something that was supposed to be God's and God's alone. It could be said that Adam and Eve gave their hearts and their relationships with God to the serpent, Satan. The case can also be made that when Satan deceived Eve, he, in effect, swindled her and subsequently Adam as well. In this way, we can say that Satan stole mankind's relationship with God.

Everything God has done since then has been to implement a plan to reconcile all of mankind to Him and re-establish the relationship lost when mankind sinned. Everything the enemy has done since then has been to keep what he stole by destroying or killing everything that has a chance of being restored to God. God and Satan have been at war since before Eden.

Jesus made this declaration about the war in the gospel of John:

> The thief comes only to steal and kill and destroy; I have come that they may have life, and have it to the full (John 10:10).

The purpose of this spiritual war, then, is for each side to win as many of us as possible. One side is fighting for our present and eternal freedom and the other side is fighting for our present and eternal captivity:

> His intent was that now, through the church, the manifold wisdom of God should be made known to the rulers and authorities in the heavenly realms, according to his eternal purpose which he accomplished in Christ Jesus our Lord. In him and through faith in him we may approach God with freedom and confidence (Ephesians 3:10–12).

It is God's will, His choice and His purpose that we can approach Him with freedom and confidence:

> But God demonstrates his own love for us in this: While we were still sinners, Christ died for us. Since we have now been justified by his blood, how much more shall we be saved from God's wrath through him! For if, when we were God's enemies, we were reconciled to him through the death of his Son, how much more, having been reconciled, shall we be saved through his life! Not only is this so, but we also rejoice in God through our Lord Jesus Christ, through whom we have now received reconciliation (Romans 5:8–10).

God determined His will, His choice and His purpose before we deserved to be considered for such a lofty privilege.

So this is what this spiritual war is all about for us: We are fighting to believe that what God wants for us is ours— His peace, joy and love; His healing, salvation and provision; His teaching, guidance and comfort.

We are the desire of God's heart. He loves us as His own, and He is not willing that we should perish.

> For God so loved the world that he gave his one and only Son, that whoever believes in him shall not perish but have eternal life (John 3:16).

> The Lord is not slow in keeping his promise, as some understand slowness. He is patient with you, not wanting anyone to perish, but everyone to come to repentance (2 Peter 3:9).

> This is how God showed his love among us: He sent his one and only Son into the world that we might live through him. This is love: not that we loved God, but that he loved us and sent his Son as an atoning sacrifice for our sins (1 John 4:19).

Satan's main objective is to gather as many to his kingdom as he can and God's main objective is gather as many to His kingdom as He can.

Any war carries with it death, destruction and difficult times. This spiritual war is no different. Just look at the news headlines today. You see stories about murder, rape, anger, fear and depression. These are the stories that we see when evil overcomes good. We also hear many stories where the opposite is true. When we hear about brave rescues, incredible generosity or the love of friends, we know good can overcome evil.

Some think about these stories and events as though they are only a part of the human condition. Others tend to think about these stories and events in the context of spiritual warfare.

Apply the idea of this good versus evil battle going on all around us to our personal lives: Think how hard it is to resist the temptations we face every day, how easy it is to do the wrong thing and how hard it is to do the right thing. Where does this temptation come from? Why does life seem so difficult sometimes? Why do we say the things we do? We don't mean to hurt others, but we do. Most of us, at one time or another, have said or done something that we regret, something that we didn't intend. It is my belief that we can often link these experiences to the spiritual world.

Are you a casualty of this war? My father used to tell a story about a man he knew named Joe. Every time my dad saw him, Joe would talk about how mad he was about something that had happened 30 years earlier. Joe was never able to get past this experience. It shaped his life every day until he died. He was bitter and angry and hard to get along with. We all know that Joe's experience, this constant state of bitterness, wasn't normal. The question is, to what extent was Joe's experience his own fault? What was happening to Joe that would cause him to stay in a constant state of anger because of an experience that occurred over 30 years ago? Would you agree that Joe might have been caught in a trap? I believe he was a victim of this spiritual war.

Here's another example of what I'm describing as spiritual war. Some time ago, I observed a young man acting in a way that made me feel like I wanted to get as far away from him as possible. I had joined with a number of single people from our church at a bible camp for a retreat. This young man was a part of our group. He was running around and teasing the young women and causing a little bit of a stir. A small group of us were watching him and someone observed that he was making a fool of himself. We all agreed, and we kept our distance from him. Over the course of the weekend, I noticed that few, if any, people were spending time with him or allowing him into their conversations.

The funny thing was, I observed another fellow doing pretty much the same thing. Rather than being disgusted, most people were laughing along with him. He was able to spend plenty of time with anyone he wanted to.

Why was there such a difference between the two men when their actions were so similar?

I think this was an observable act of spiritual warfare for the first young man. He was subject to some kind of "law" that kept him imprisoned and trapped by rejection. Everything he did to become accepted caused him to be rejected again. When he was teasing the girls he was trying to be accepted. Yet the very thing he was doing to be accepted was causing him to be rejected.

People who have suffered real, painful rejection can become stuck in this kind of cycle. The cycle is difficult to break. Like this young man, they make choices over and over again that cause further rejection. It's hard to understand. The people around him should have been more accepting, and he should have been easier to accept. Yet it seemed like the cycle might not ever be broken.

If you have been caught in a cycle like this, whether it was (or is) a cycle of rejection or something else, you know that it is difficult to get free from it. You try everything in your power to be free, but it feels futile. It's as though there is some kind of force keeping you in the cycle. You can't put your finger on it, but it doesn't seem right. It's almost as though there is some kind of law being enforced, something outside of your control that keeps you stuck in the trap.

This is why we're going to learn how to fight. This is why we're going to learn how to use weapons that will help us find freedom from cycles of pain and traps that keep us from fulfilling God's plan. This is what Christ died for. To release us from captivity. We will learn how and why to practice thankfulness, personal worship of God and honoring and forgiving the people in our lives. We will learn how these simple acts of spiritual war will lead us to our personal deliverance.

These weapons and principles are the tools we need to gain our freedom. We can get there. We just need to start practicing the simplest of spiritual weapons.

Chapter 2

Enemy Tactics

Many Christians are aware that Satan exists and that he has influence on people. Most are not aware of his primary tactics, neither are they aware of the great numbers of people impacted by his activity. It is scary, in a kind of horror movie way, to think about demon possession, which is what we often consider to be the prime activity of the enemy. Yet, the activity of the enemy that has the most impact is to set a trap for you, catch you in it and ensnare you in a cycle of pain and despair. These cycles, or traps, keep you from knowing the love, peace and joy of the Lord on a consistent basis. They could include worry, frustration, insecurity and selfishness. Whatever the cycles are, being trapped in them feels very real.

My friend Louise seemed to be stuck in one of these traps or cycles. She had been a teacher in a small country school for nearly twenty years. Her students loved her and were glad to have her as their teacher. When it came to getting along with her co-workers, though, sometimes it was a different story.

One day she wore a new outfit to school. As she was walking to her classroom she met Sue, one of the newer teachers at the school. They spoke for a moment before Sue said to Louise that she thought her skirt was cute. Louise had a fit. She took great offense to the comment and told Sue about it right then and there. Louise, telling me about the experience later, said, "I put her in her place!"

Louise thought Sue was attacking her and she said things to her that were hurtful and uncalled for as she defended herself. She offended Sue in her overreaction. On its own, this incident might not be considered a spiritual attack. Maybe Louise was having a bad day. Maybe Sue really did mean something snide by what she said.

Yet, the pervasive, repetitive nature of this kind of interaction with people by Louise suggests that Satan did have something to do with it. He had something to do with it, at least in the very early stages, to help her establish a belief that she had something to be insecure about. Every time she felt that kind of insecurity, her fierce defense caused a great deal of pain and agony for whoever crossed her and made her feel insecure.

Once the ball started rolling, the enemy didn't have too much work to do to keep it rolling. Her very actions and statements about herself contributed to maintaining an attitude or 'spirit' of fear. Every time she felt afraid, she would react in a similar way. In this way, she unwittingly played along with the enemy exactly as he planned.

When Louise did receive counseling and deliverance ministry for this problem, the counseling and the ministry neglected the simple lessons we are learning here. Her counselors failed to put weapons in her hands that she could practice wielding in her own defense, not from those who said things that hurt her, but from the one who was the source of that hurting.

Had she grasped the truth, that she had nothing to be afraid of, she would have found that the truth would set her free from being afraid. She had nothing to be insecure about. Everyone who knew her thought Louise was bright and intelligent and very gifted in art. But she would never embrace what God gave her as being sufficient. In fact, she became rather manipulative in her insecurity, asking for validation about things that she either couldn't change or that she knew to be perfectly fine. When she asked, "How do I look?" there was only one right answer. When she talked about her paintings she would say, "I'm afraid to show my art, because someone might not like it." She asked these kinds of questions and made these statements so frequently that sometimes it was difficult to be around her.

All this because she didn't know the basic skills of fighting the enemy: *How to become thankful, establish a personal worship connection with the Lord, and how to honor and forgive the people in her life.* So when she sought help with the difficulties she faced and worked with people who helped her find some freedom, it wasn't long before she became stuck in the same trap. The spiritual warfare she received help with was actually somewhat ineffective, because she would talk herself right back to the place of insecurity she started from before she had ministry.

Louise was never taught how to avoid the battle, let alone how to win it. We can learn very simple ways of recognizing the snares and traps the enemy uses to ambush us. And, if we've been caught in one of those traps or snares we can learn how to escape. We don't have to become a casualty of a spiritual battle. We can live the life Christ died and rose again for us to have. All we need to do is learn how to fight.

Most of us don't know how to fight. If we knew how to fight, how to prevent or avoid attacks and recognize when the fight is on, we could experience greater victory in our lives. We could have greater peace. We could love others better and more freely worship our God. We would be better equipped to come to the aid of friends and family when they are under attack because we would know what to do.

Consider the movie, "The Exorcist." Regan, the main character, is demon-possessed and the attempts to deliver her are awful. The consequence of thinking about Satan like we see him in this kind of movie or hear about him in stories is that we think he is always trying to fight us head-on in full force.

The reality is that a full head-on confrontation with Satan is fairly rare. Even in the Garden of Eden, Satan did not attack Eve with physical violence. It was the same with Jesus. In both of these cases, the attack was subtle and deceptive in its nature.

Satan and his forces are at work to take advantage of our weaknesses. If we fail to recognize the enemy's battle plan, we'll stay trapped. Are we angry? We rehearse the reasons we should stay angry. Are we afraid? We worry and fret so that we stay afraid. Are we rejected? We tell ourselves that no one loves us, and we continue to feel rejected.

We blame others for our problems. We develop reasons and rationale for staying in the state we are trapped in. We continue to be angry, refuse to take responsibility and worry about improbable things. In effect, we do all the work it takes to stay in the trap the enemy has caught us in.

If you think about it for a second, Satan doesn't have to work too hard to make our lives miserable. All he has to do is get us to agree that our lives are miserable, and we will take care of the rest.

It could be that your car broke down and you decided that your life was hard and you wondered, "Why me, God?"

You just stepped into the snare. Maybe my wife didn't have dinner ready on time, and I thought, "She doesn't care about me, so I don't care about her." I just stepped into a trap.

What would you feel if your husband lost his job? Would you be afraid? Ungrateful? Angry? You could be at risk for stepping into a trap. The last time you said something you regretted, what did you feel? Rejected? Worried? Indignant? You may have been caught in a snare.

Satan is capable of instigating great evil in the world and in our personal lives. We have to make a decision about how we will act with regard to what we know, and this is what we know: We have power over Satan when we stand in Christ on His Word and use the authority of His Name.

We are mostly ignorant of how to use that power. We know that we are vulnerable to Satan's ways if we are not being diligent in guarding ourselves against him. We are unable to defeat the enemy on our own. Our lives are evidence that we lose battles to him daily. But, *in Christ we have the victory*, and the more skilled we become at using the simple weapons of spiritual warfare, the more we will see His victory in our lives.

Satan's objective is to do whatever he can to ruin us. Satan has a plan to accomplish his objective. In various Bible searches I have found that there are at least 40 biblical uses of the word **"snare"** and 25 uses of the word **"trap."** So, while there are references in the Bible to direct demonic confrontation, there are at least as many references to this more subtle kind of warfare. Setting snares and traps is an efficient and effective way of capturing and rendering ineffective the prey that you are seeking.

The United States was first explored and settled by trappers and hunters. Trappers would set out the trap line and then go back to their camp and drink coffee and eat flapjacks. After a couple of days, they would go out and check the trap line they set. They would look at every trap. When they found one that didn't catch their prey, they would bait it again and maybe move it a little. When they found one that had caught the prey, but it wasn't dead yet, they would beat the animal to death so as to preserve the pelt.

Isn't this the way it is for us? We go about our lives secure in the way things are. We're not worried about traps or snares. We're not worried about trouble. All of a sudden everything changes. We had a bad experience. We saw something we shouldn't have. We heard about something that caught our attention. We're tempted. Tempted to drink or spend too much time on the Internet. We're tempted to stay angry or become afraid. After all, we have good reason, don't we?

We wake up one morning and we think, "How did I get here? How did I get stuck? How come this place hurts so much? Why do I feel like I'm trapped?"

If we allow ourselves to stay in the trap too long, we get used to it. Sometimes we forget we're in the trap at all. Many of us have learned to live pretty well with traps and snares. We can go about our daily business most of the time and as far as we know, we're doing fine. But then we see something happen in our life. We remember that we've been through this before. This is the second or third time we've lost our job because our boss is unreasonable or disrespectful. Or we just had another car accident. Or we're having another dramatic episode with one of our friends. Now that we think about it, these kinds of things seem to happen to us over and over again.

We can explain the isolated incidents. Everyone has a rough day now and then. But when we're observing a pattern in our own lives or in the lives of people we care about, we can say that the idea of being caught in a trap or a snare explains the problem pretty well.

Once we're in the trap and we recognize it, we want to get out, to be set free. We want to be free to actually have peace at our jobs and in our relationships, so we can live the way we were meant to live. We want to be able to walk in the purpose for which God created us.

David understood this idea. He wrote about traps and snares and miry pits in his psalms of praise to the Lord. In these psalms, David described the enemy's tactics and called him a fowler (A fowler catches birds in snares.), a pit digger and a trap setter:

> Surely he will save you from the fowler's snare
> and from the deadly pestilence (Psalm 91:3).
>
> He also brought me up out of a horrible pit,
> Out of the miry clay,
> And set my feet upon a rock,
> And established my steps (Psalm 40:2).
>
> My eyes are ever on the Lord, for only he will
> release my feet from the snare (Ps 25:15).

Paul explained these kinds of tactics by using the example of a stronghold:

> The weapons we fight with are not the weapons of
> the world. On the contrary, they have divine power
> to demolish strongholds (2 Corinthians 10:4 NIV).

The dictionary defines the term stronghold as a well-fortified place, a fortress. Strong's *Exhaustive Concordance (#G3794)* offers similar definitions for the word stronghold:

- a castle, stronghold, fortress, fastness
- anything on which one relies
- of the arguments and reasonings by which a disputant endeavours to fortify his opinion and defend it against his opponent

The use of "stronghold" might make you think about a fort or castle built to keep enemies from coming in and wreaking havoc. The image Paul is getting at is more like a prison.

Strongholds do two things: They keep people and things in, and they keep people and things out. These strongholds keep us from moving ahead to maturity and finding deliverance from the trouble we face that we never seem to be able to get away from. Satan uses strongholds to keep you in, not let you out. Letting you out, that is, setting you free, is what the mighty weapons of our warfare do.

With that in mind, let's look at something Jesus said that relates to Paul's picture of a stronghold:

> And I tell you that you are Peter, and on this rock I will build my church, and the gates of Hades will not overcome it (Matthew 16:18).

Jesus said that the gates of hell would not overcome His church. I had a hard time understanding what He meant by this until I thought of a horse corral. A horse corral has a gate. The purpose of a horse corral and its gate is to keep the horse in, not to keep anything out. I thought about what Satan would really like to do to the church. If he were able to keep the church hemmed in, unable to go out and perform the tasks assigned to it or accomplish the purposes it was created for, then that would help him accomplish his purpose.

When Jesus says that the gates of hell shall not prevail against the church and Paul says our weapons are not man-made but are mighty to pull down strongholds, I am convinced that we are equipped to get out of the traps and snares and pits and strongholds that have held us in for so long. We can see this elsewhere in the Word in every place we see an instruction or encouragement to overcome our circumstances. John writes in his first letter: "…for everyone born of God overcomes the world. This is the victory that has overcome the world, even our faith. Who is it that overcomes the world? Only he who believes that Jesus is the Son of God (I John 5:4-5).

There is another tactic of the enemy we should be aware of. Peter identified it in the following passage:

> Be self-controlled and alert. Your enemy the devil prowls around like a roaring lion looking for someone to devour (1 Peter 5:8).

I have learned, mostly through watching nature shows on PBS, about the way lions hunt. Lions, as big and powerful as they are, do not attack the middle of the herds of musk oxen and gnus when they hunt. Instead, they look for the weak, the sick and the old. They look for isolated animals that are not able to keep up with the herd. It's the same for us. The enemy looks for those who are isolated from fellowship whether by fear or some other reason. That's why it is important for you to surround yourself with people you can trust, who are willing to tell you the truth when you ask for help, and who can help you when you need it.

We know we have an enemy who intends bad things for us. It can be intimidating to think about if we believe we're alone and that we have no weapons or power to help us win the battle we face. It would be unfortunate to focus on how the enemy fights and completely miss an examination of where we stand in this war.

A careful examination of the Word shows us that we are neither alone nor without weapons or power. We have the great blessing of knowing the outcome before we can see it with our own eyes. We are the victors! Listen to this description of victory in Revelation:

> They overcame him by the blood of the Lamb and by the word of their testimony; they did not love their lives so much as to shrink from death (Revelation 12:11).

Notice who the overcomers are: **We are the ones who overcome the enemy**. It's not the other way around. Satan does not overcome us. We overcome him. Look closer. Not only is the enemy somehow beaten, he is beaten by our acts of war, namely our testimony. Our victory is secured by the blood of the Lamb and walked out by the word of our testimony.

It is critical that we understand the impact of what we say when we are in the middle of a battle. When we give thanks in a situation that seems to demand ungratefulness, when we personally connect with God in worship and when we honor the people in our lives, even the ones who may be making it difficult, this is the testimony that overcomes the enemy.

Jesus has given us authority over the enemy. This authority gives our weapons power:

When the seventy-two disciples returned, they joyfully reported to him, "Lord, even the demons obey us when we use your name!" "Yes," he told them, "I saw Satan fall from heaven like lightning! Look, I have given you authority over all the power of the enemy, and you can walk among snakes and scorpions and crush them. Nothing will injure you" (Luke 10:17-18).

The Word indicates that we have the advantage over the enemy. Our advantage in this war rests entirely in Christ. It is His shed blood, His death and His resurrection that have won the battle for us. It is our work and purpose to apply His victory to our own lives when we are under the attack of our spiritual enemy. As He said, "I have given you all authority."

I think we have been poorly taught when it comes to spiritual warfare and its impact on our Christian walk. We clearly don't need to be afraid of Satan. At the same time there is little reason for arrogance. There is too much we don't know about him to disrespect him. He and his minions are behind every evil thing that has ever happened. What he has done in the earth and on the earth through man's complicity with his desires is almost unfathomable in terms of both the loss of human life and quality of human life.

So while we will spend some time confirming that we needn't be afraid, we must not lose respect for the enemy to the extent that we forget what he can do. Think of him like the water in a lake or an ocean. You don't have to be afraid of the water, even though it's not a good idea to lose respect for what it can do under certain conditions. So don't be afraid. But do take precaution against the worst case. Learn the use of the simple weapons of war and always have them with you. Then when you encounter difficult circumstances, you will be able to defeat the enemy and avoid his traps and snares.

Satan's defeat by Christ means we don't have to be afraid. Jesus Himself declares the great result of Satan's defeat in Revelation 1:18:

> "I am the Living One; I was dead, and behold I am alive forever and ever! And I hold the keys of death and Hades."

It is clear in the Scriptures that we are in Christ:

- Therefore, there is now no condemnation for those who are *in Christ Jesus* (Romans 8:1).
- It is because of him that you are *in Christ Jesus*… (1 Corinthians 1:30).
- Therefore, if anyone is *in Christ*, he is a new creation… (2 Corinthians 5:17).
- We have been speaking in the sight of God as those *in Christ*… (2 Corinthians 12:19).
- But now *in Christ Jesus* you who once were far away have been brought near through the blood of Christ (Ephesians 2:13).
- That I may gain Christ and *be found in him*, not having a righteousness of my own… (Philippians 3:9).
    All verses with my emphasis

If we are in Christ, then it must also be true that we have the same victory as He does. Yet, we often live in such defeat. Somehow we have failed to establish a connection within us to Christ's victory, and we remain connected to our defeat at the hand of the enemy. If we haven't understood how to connect with the victory that Christ has won for us, then we can only *see* the victory instead of *living* in the victory.

Jesus has beaten Satan on his own ground and taken the most valuable possessions the enemy had. Those were the keys of death and hell. If Jesus holds the keys to death and hell, then it stands to reason that we have nothing to be afraid of. You have already been delivered from these things. How much more have you been delivered from everything that leads to death and hell?

I repeat: You have nothing to fear.

You may have to fight. You may have to press into the Lord for your growth and your deliverance. It may be more work than you anticipated, but you surely have nothing to fear from the enemy.

Every day you walk through events and experiences that contain traps and snares. To one extent or another, you have been caught in some of these traps and snares. Knowing these primary tactics of the enemy should help you overcome some of the fear you've brought into your understanding of spiritual warfare. If you know that the enemy wants to trap you or imprison you within walls he helps you create (strongholds), the idea of it is not so scary or mysterious. In fact, if you learn how to pay attention, it will be pretty hard for the enemy to accomplish his objective. If he can't attain his objective, then it will be hard for him to keep you from accomplishing what God has given you to do.

> For our struggle is not against flesh and blood, but against the rulers, against the authorities, against the powers of this dark world and against the spiritual forces of evil in the heavenly realms (Ephesians 6:12).

It is my belief that, having this understanding, you can begin to look at our life and circumstances with more confidence in God and His Word. You can be less afraid of what you think the enemy is going to do, or could do, or is able to do. And you can begin to use your status as God's child to grow and mature and become smarter about how you engage in this war.

You can begin to believe that victory is possible!

Chapter 3

What Are You Saying in Your Heart?

One day some time ago I called a friend I was just getting to know to see if I could spend a little bit of time talking to him about life in general. My real purpose was to spend some time with him complaining about my life. Not big complaints, mind you, just some basic whining about why God wasn't giving me more direction and how some of my co-workers were hard to work with.

My friend didn't have time for me.

No big deal, right? Of course it wasn't. Later that night, I went to bed and I was thinking about my friend's lack of interest and time for me. I said to the Lord, "Why can't I just find someone to gripe and complain with once in awhile?" I heard Him say back to me, "Why can't you gripe and complain with me?"

This is so memorable for me because I felt the Lord saying He cares enough to listen to me talk about my troubles. True, it is clear in His Word that He doesn't want me to complain bitterly and wallow in unhappiness. But that night it became clear that He was interested in the kind of intimacy that I was looking for. He wanted to be my friend. He wanted me to talk to Him about the same things I had planned on talking to someone else about. He wanted to help me sort out legitimate complaints from whining. He wanted me then, and He wants me now, to come to Him when I am unhappy and let Him know what I am unhappy about. In other words,

He wants me to talk to Him about my life. He *is* interested in me and *everything* that is in my heart. This is true for you as well. He *is* interested in you and *everything* that is in your heart.

Jesus spoke of our hearts many times when He was on earth. In Matthew, Mark and Luke he says we should love the Lord our God with all our heart, our soul, our mind and our strength. The Greek word used in the Gospels for heart is "kardia." Strong's Exhaustive Concordance (G2588) defines kardia as "…the center and seat of spiritual life: the soul or mind, as it is the fountain and seat of the thoughts, passions, desires, appetites, affections, purposes, endeavors…of the will and character."

The nature of my heart is exposed by my reactions to the daily occurrences in my life. I know how I am reacting to them by listening to what I say in my heart about them.

These occurrences happen at work, with my wife and friends, with my children and, frequently, when I am driving around town in traffic. Christ's objective for taking an interest in me is to help me form a proper heart. He wants me to evaluate what I am saying in my heart so that, with the help of the Holy Spirit, I can change it.

Once we've asked Jesus to come into our heart and we accept Him as Lord and Savior we become the new man in our spirits (See Ephesians 4:22-24). Unfortunately for us, the internal change that happens in our spirits through the act of being born again must work its way through to the external. Therein lies the rub.

In the previous chapter we talked about the enemy's tactics. We learned that one of his tactics is to set traps for us. Where does he set his traps? It may look like he sets them all around us in the form of what we might call the things of this world: going to bars and parties, sexual temptations, love of money, etc. But I wonder if he sets these traps in our hearts more frequently. James wrote about this.

> …but each one is tempted when, by his own evil desire, he is dragged away and enticed. Then, after desire has conceived, it gives birth to sin; and sin, when it is full-grown, gives birth to death (James 1:14 -15).

James is not talking about the enemy physically dragging you away and enticing you. But it is a good picture of what happens when you are tempted in your heart and dragged away from the peace and love of Christ to be become angry and stay bitter, or become worried and afraid, for example.

Satan is pretty good at taking advantage of what is already in your hearts and trapping you with it. He baits the trap with whatever he thinks will entice you. You begin to say things in your heart about the events of the day. How will you decide to deal with stress or success? How will you deal with pain? Will you talk yourself into becoming angry or bitter about something that happened yesterday or today? Will that lead to an outburst that hurts other people (and you)? Will you have one too many glasses of wine to celebrate, or search the Internet for something that will ultimately cause you even more pain? Will you choose to leave the peace of Christ to become anxious and afraid by what you say? What you say in your heart about your circumstances will lead you into or out of a trap. What you say will either build the stronghold that keeps you captive or demolish the stronghold so you can be free.

So there is a purpose for God's desire for a closer intimacy, a deeper relationship. He wants you to share with Him what is in your heart. What is in your heart and what you say about it is what determines whether you will be able to fulfill the plan He has made for you. What is in your heart impacts your ability to worship God and it impacts the success of your relationships with the people in your life. His purpose is that your heart is exposed in order for Him to have access to fix it. When you tell Him about your trials and your tribulations, you expose your heart to Him. If you expose your heart to Him in an attitude of humility and allow Him to teach you, it is possible to change what is in your heart. If what is in your heart can change, then your experience can change, and you will be better able to fulfill the plan He has made for you.

Let's think of some examples of decisions people make in their hearts. The decision we made for Christ was made in our hearts. The decision I made to marry my wife and love her was made in my heart. We've been married for nearly 24 years, and we've hit the occasional bumps in the road that many people experience. During some of those rough times I have been tempted to say in my heart "I can't live with her," but I chose not to say it. I have always chosen to say in my heart that I think she is beautiful, that I am blessed to have her as my wife and that I love her. I don't love every little thing she does, and she doesn't love every little thing I do. Had I chosen to tell myself over and over again what I didn't like about our marriage, my life would probably be different by now. I might have allowed little problems in our marriage to grow into big problems in our marriage. But I have chosen *not* to cultivate what I *don't* like by *not* thinking and talking to myself about those things and growing them in my heart. I make heart decisions about my children and about my friends in the same kinds of ways.

On the other hand, I have made decisions in my heart to like or not like a boss, to say, "I can work with her" or "I can't work with him." Other decisions I have made that have had long-lasting negative impacts on me have to do with how I decided to think about my childhood. I thought I would never be good enough to be loved. I was unhappy with my parents. I decided to rebel against them. I felt like I was in trouble all the time. I decided to lie and be sneaky so that I wouldn't get in trouble. I wanted people to know I was smart. I became arrogant. Those decisions and thoughts became things I said in my heart. The more I said those things in my heart the more they became a part of me. The things I said in my heart helped me rationalize every action I took in rebellion. The thoughts I had about my parents were easily transferred to my managers and supervisors. The things I said in my heart when I was a child kept me from making positive decisions about my jobs and my bosses as an adult.

These heart decisions guided my steps and paths. They guide your steps and your paths, too. Much of the time the decisions you make in your heart influence your experience in this life. You choose to be angry or forgiving. You choose to be thankful. You choose to be unhappy and ungrateful. You choose to overcome or to be overcome by circumstance.

Suppose something happens today that hurts your feelings. As you think about what happened, you have several choices as to how you might react. These choices are happening in both your mind and your heart

You begin by thinking about the event. You process it as objectively as you can (with varying degrees of success) and you begin to draw conclusions. Maybe you think it is your fault; maybe someone else is to blame. You think about all of the possible responses you should have made or could have made. You think about all of the possible responses you can make now that you have processed the experience. During this time you are using your brain for thought while at the same time you are processing the feelings in your heart. Your heart may be nearly bursting with emotion. You could be angry, afraid or deeply wounded. You may know in your mind that you should walk in forgiveness and peace and love. But, your heart may lead you to determine that you will remain angry or hurt or afraid.

If you decide to remain angry, then you will say things in your heart that foster on-going anger. The same will happen if you decide to remain hurt or afraid. Every time you think about this experience, these feelings will be renewed. Every time you agree with the thoughts and feelings, you add to the walls of the stronghold being built in your heart.

Does this mean that you should never say you are angry or hurt or afraid? No, I don't think so. But Christ's work for us holds a better plan. It offers you the opportunity to find freedom from these feelings and escape from the strongholds you've built with the things you have said in your heart. You may have spent years building these strongholds. You believe what you've said and you believe that you made the right decision. You have come to have faith in this stronghold because you have continued to say in your heart that you are right to feel this way. The problem is that you have developed and grown your faith in the wrong place. Your stronghold has become your place of faith.

To grow in your walk with God and overcome the difficulties you face you have to come to grips with the fact that faith is the basic building block of your entire life.

> And without faith it is impossible to please God, because anyone who comes to him must believe that he exists and that he rewards those who earnestly seek him (Hebrews 11:6).

It is your faith in God and His love for you that gives you the chance to become thankful, to establish a deeper relationship with God through personal worship, and honor and forgive the people in your life. The difficult thing about Paul's statement is how it reaches down into what you believe as opposed to how you act. It is not your behavior that makes you pleasing to God. Your behavior has never made you pleasing to God. Furthermore, it is clear from the scriptures that you have done nothing to earn God's love.

We love because He first loved us (1 John 4:19).

The Word is clear that you won't gain access to heaven because you are good. Paul emphasizes this in his letter to the Galatians. "I do not set aside the grace of God, for if righteousness could be gained through the law, Christ died for nothing!" (Galatians 2:21). In other words, it can't be your behavior that earns God's love, because if it were possible that your behavior could earn God's love it would mean that Christ's death and resurrection would be unimportant and insignificant. You and I both know that idea can't be right.

Does this mean that you and I can do anything we want? No. Our behavior should change for the better when we become Christians. At the same time, we want that change in behavior to be generated from within our hearts as a result of growth in our relationship with God rather than our effort to perform to an external standard.

Growing into a mature Christian requires that you look into your heart and judge what you are saying in your heart to answer this question: "Is my behavior cause-focused rather than effect-focused?" In circumstances that you find difficult, are you identifying the effect of your decisions and the things you say? Or, are you justifying your decisions and the things you say as though they are caused by something else?

Let's say you have a hard time holding a job, for example. You may think there are several causes for your situation. Maybe you think no one wants you to succeed. Or maybe you think you are under attack from the enemy. You may think of many reasons why you can't hold a job, but they may have nothing to do with your own shortcomings. If this is the case, there are all kinds of things you can do to try to fix the problem, but none of them will have lasting effect. Because what is required to change your circumstance is to make a change in you.

All of your actions and behaviors have not helped you hold a job long enough to support yourself or your family. The only thing that will produce change in your situation will be the decision you make in your heart to change yourself. This change you make within your self is what will be pleasing to God. The behavior that changes your heart is the correction of what you have been saying in your heart about your situation, about your circumstance. You must make a decision in your heart that what you have thought and said about your circumstance up to this point has been wrong. You may have identified the facts of your situation correctly, but the decisions you have made may have led you into a trap or built a stronghold that is keeping you from the victory God has provided for you.

To escape this stronghold, you must replace ungratefulness with thankfulness. You must find a way to honor and respect the people whom you have dishonored and disrespected by what you have said about them. You must find a way to establish your worship connection with the Lord. These are the actions you can take to bring change into your life and your circumstance.

To learn how to change your circumstance and grow in your relationship with God you have to begin to recognize what you are saying in our heart about everything. What you're saying about God, your spouse and your children. About your parents, brothers and sisters. About your pastors. Then you have to begin to correct what you are saying in your heart so that you can overcome your circumstance through growth in your heart rather than growth in your brain.

It's not that you don't have to use your intellect. You use your intellect to evaluate what you are saying and compare it to what the Word says. Your intellect helps you identify and evaluate what you need to change. Your intellect provides you with information and judgment so that you can make a decision in your heart to make that change.

Some time ago there was a commercial on TV that sort of gets at what I'm talking about. Every scene would begin with someone asking the question, "How are you?" Instead of simply responding with "I'm fine" or "Okay," the response from the other person was an in-depth and sometimes gross description about whatever it was that ailed them.   In one of the commercials a man was about to order a meal at a fast-food place, and the server asked through the intercom, "How are you today?" The man proceeded to tell the server all the details about his cold and fever and diarrhea. He didn't hide anything. He exposed his experience to the poor, unfortunate person who asked them the question.

You and I wouldn't normally give this kind of answer when we're asked, "How are you doing?" Sometimes, you aren't doing fine and you still don't tell anyone, because maybe you are afraid or insecure. Maybe you don't trust the person you are talking with. Maybe you're angry or hurt. Whatever your true experience is, you respond by saying "Great! How are you?" It's when you're alone, thinking about your circumstance and your experience, that what is in your heart really comes out. That is when you talk with yourself about your bitterness, your anger and your pain. That is when you talk with yourself about what you really believe about God. Have you ever said these things either in your heart or out loud?

>"God doesn't really care about me."
>"Why did You put me here?"
>"Why can't I ever get past this?"

Here are some examples of common words we say both out loud and in our hearts that seem to cement negative things for us: "I'll never...." "She'll never..." "He always..." "This is the worst...." "Why doesn't anyone care?" "I'll never forgive her for..." "He is always..."

At that very moment when you are saying these things *and* you hear them, you have two choices. You can continue to say these things in your heart and perpetuate your negative, painful experience. Or you can bring these experiences and feelings to the Lord and ask the Holy Spirit to teach you how to overcome these statements you have made in our hearts.

The statements you make in our hearts about your circumstance and experience are a direct reflection of what you believe. If you say that you can never forgive a person who has hurt you, you begin to build faith in that statement and make forgiveness harder to do. If you say that you can forgive a person, even if it hurts, you may find that the pain is short lived. The peace you lost when you were hurt is then able to come in and replace your pain, and God's love can then soothe your hurt and anger. The inward change in your heart will begin to find its way to your outward action.

What does the Word say about all these things? How do you know that what you say in your heart is important and that you should pay attention to it?

> They overcame him by the blood of the Lamb and by the word of their testimony...(Revelation 12:11)

> **For thou hast said in thine heart**, I will ascend into heaven, I will exalt my throne above the stars of God: I will sit also upon the mount of the congregation, in the sides of the north: 14 I will ascend above the heights of the clouds; I will be like the most High. (Isaiah 14:13-14 KJV emphasis mine)

Pay attention to this most important fact: It was what Satan said in his heart that led him to rebel against God. He made statements in his heart over and over again until he believed them. He continued saying them until he began to act on them. As he continued to say these things to himself, they became his testimony. His false testimony, what he said in his heart, ultimately caused his downfall.

Imagine what it might have been like for Satan. He had a passing thought, "I am just like God." Maybe he was shocked at the thought at first. The thought came again. It wasn't quite as shocking this time. He pondered it for a second and then said, "No. I can't think like that." And then again and again. The next thing he knew he was pursuing the thought. He was reaching out for it and stirring it up. He became what he thought by continuing to think about it and making it part of his nature. The thought became a defining characteristic of who he is.

Likewise the tongue is a small part of the body, but it makes great boasts. Consider what a great forest is set on fire by a small spark. The tongue also is a fire, a world of evil among the parts of the body. It corrupts the whole person, sets the whole course of his life on fire, and is itself set on fire by hell (James 3:5-6).

"Make a tree good and its fruit will be good, or make a tree bad and its fruit will be bad, for a tree is recognized by its fruit. You brood of vipers, how can you who are evil say anything good? For out of the overflow of the heart the mouth speaks. The good man brings good things out of the good stored up in him, and the evil man brings evil things out of the evil stored up in him. But I tell you that men will have to give account on the Day of Judgment for every careless word they have spoken (Matthew 12:33-36).

The Greek word for overflow used in Matthew 12:34 is defined as the abundance "…in which one delights…of that which fills the heart." (See Strong's Exhaustive Concordance #G4051)

This is really the question you must answer: How do you know what is in your heart?

"Out of the abundance of the heart…" Out of the abundance in which one delights, out of that which fills the heart. What does your heart delight in? Really, what does your heart delight in? Does it delight in complaining? Does it delight in its pain? Is it envy? Is it bitterness? How would you know if something like these things did fill you heart?

I watch some reality TV shows with my family. We are always amazed at the things people say to each other when they are under stress. It's surprising to see the mistakes they make when the stress is great enough to cloud their judgment. On *Survivor*, people are taken way out into the wilderness for 39 days. They are left with little resources, and they're required to compete in physically taxing competitions for the chance to stay in the game. At the end of every competition someone from the losing team is voted off the island. No one can hide from who they really are under those kinds of conditions. If you want to see a live demonstration of what we are discussing here, reality TV will give you an opportunity.

It's when you're under stress, when you're afraid or you've been hurt that you can see and hear what is really in your heart. These are the times when you cry out, "Why me, God?" You say things that reveal what is really in your heart. Are you blaming your husband or your wife for this problem? Or your parents? Or your friend or pastor? Or your boss or co-worker? What do you most often say in your heart when things are going badly for you?

If you can begin to listen to what you say in the worst of times, you can begin to identify the traps and snares that are keeping you locked in this cycle of pain and trouble. Once you've identified these traps and snares you can change what you're saying in your heart. As you begin to change what you are saying in your heart you will experience more success in overcoming your trials and tribulations. You will find that you are able to grow in your relationship with God and with others in ways you didn't think possible. When you change what you say in your heart about these trials and tribulations, it will be easier for you to hear God. You'll be able to allow Him to work in your heart and in your situation to bring you freedom.

Here's an example of what I mean. One day, I was talking with some co-workers and we were laughing about the story of the day. As usual, I was laughing the loudest. My boss came down the hall and yelled at me for being so loud. I was offended, of course. On the way home from work I was rehearsing the event and thinking of what I should have said and what I should say the next time that happened. None of this was going in a positive direction. I was thinking about how I wouldn't let him talk to me that way and how he shouldn't be so sensitive and how people know about laughter, etc, etc., etc. And then I had a thought. I remembered that my boss owned the company and that I worked there at his good pleasure.

I had been saying in my heart that he was a jerk and that he had no right to talk to me the way he did. When I realized what I was saying about who he was, I stopped. I made a decision to change what I was saying in my heart.

I said to the Lord, "I am sorry I got so angry. I am sorry that I took offense at my boss's remarks. Lord, I forgive my boss for hurting me. I choose not to be bitter. Will you help me?" And then I began to say, "If my boss wants me to be quieter, then I will be more quiet. I understand that this is his business. and he can run it any way he wants to."

I had been headed into a trap. I was beginning to say things in my heart that would have led me to take actions that would cause me trouble. When I heard what I was saying in my heart I stopped. I made a decision to say something different. I was able to avoid becoming entangled in the trap when I changed what I was saying in my heart.

The next day I went to see my boss and told him I was sorry for being so loud. Even though I no longer work for this man, we are still friends. I left his company in good standing and we are both glad we had the experience of working together.

What you say in your heart about your circumstances, your feelings, the people around you and even what you say about God can lead you into or out of a bad circumstance. If you can begin to say the truth about your circumstances and the truth about God, you will surely find release from the traps and snares that have held you for so long. You will finally be able to make the changes in your life that you have desired to make for a long time.

Chapter 4

To Tell the Truth

To the Jews who had believed him, Jesus said, "If you hold to my teaching, you are really my disciples. Then you will know the truth, and the truth will set you free" (John 8:31-32).

In order to believe that there is deliverance from the problems we encounter in our daily lives, we have to establish a scriptural basis on which to build that belief. When we can establish both the basis for belief, and the starting point for implementing the plan we will be able to answer the question, "Where is deliverance?"

Many of us know the scripture so well, it's almost like a cliché: "The truth will set you free." Unfortunately, many have failed to grasp the magnitude of this declaration of deliverance. And many lack the will to pursue that deliverance to its perfect end.

If there is a mistake we frequently make in our walk with Christ, it is that we fail to act because we have somehow gotten the idea that we are passive participants in God's plan for us. Nothing could be further from the truth. Even Adam and Eve were active in what the Lord's will and purpose was for them before the fall. If anything, after the fall, we are required to be even more active in our walk.

It is very important that you make a decision to fight for your deliverance now rather than waiting for someone to bring it to you. If you truly desire deliverance from the

48

traps and snares that have entangled you, it is your responsibility to make the decision that you have had enough captivity. You have to decide that you will begin seeking deliverance from your circumstances and problems and issues right now.

Listen to the testimonies of men and women who have been delivered from drugs and addictions. Listen to the testimony of a person who has been through unimaginably tough times and found victory. Ultimately, what you hear through the story is a coming to grips with the truth. Once the truth has been embraced and spoken, then love can come in and perform its work of healing.

Without truth, love can't be enough. We all know someone who can't get enough love. We could stand beside them 24 hours a day and tell them we love them over and over again and it wouldn't be enough. They wouldn't believe it. Because they've been hurt and they've decided to hold on to that hurt rather than let it go, at best they can only hold on to love for brief moments. They are like pitchers with holes in them. Instead of holding water to be poured out when it is wanted and needed, the pitcher leaks it right out before it can fulfill its purpose and the water can be of use to anyone else.

Jesus talked about truth and its work:

> To the Jews who had believed him, Jesus said, "If you hold to my teaching, you are really my disciples. Then you will know the truth, and the truth will set you free." (John 8:31-32).

If what Jesus told the Jews was true 2000 years ago, it is true for us today.

If what Jesus said was true then, *and* it is true today, then we must establish that we are his disciples if the truth is to set us free. How can we establish that we are his disciples? If we are reading His Word and praying and fellowshipping with other believers we are at least moving in the right direction to become his disciples. The degree to which we are really His disciples is more a function of how well we hold to his teaching. The real measure of this is in what He called the greatest commandment: To love God and to love our neighbors as ourselves.

"Then you will know the truth and the truth will set you free." If you know the truth of His love for you, expressed in the cross and the power of His resurrection, you can feel safe in telling Him all of your troubles and sins. You can tell Him the truth about your life. These two things go hand-in-hand. The teachings of Christ reveal His love for you. You can feel safe enough to tell Him the truth about your life because you believe in His love. You repent because you trust that he will forgive you: If we confess our sins, he is faithful and just and will forgive us our sins and purify us from all unrighteousness (See I John 1:9). And you'll find the freedom His death and resurrection provide.

In the scriptures below we find that the Lord desires us to tell Him the truth. The truth He desires is the truth in our hearts. His offer to us is greater intimacy and closer living with Him when we tell him the truth about our lives from our hearts.

> LORD, who may dwell in your sanctuary?
> Who may live on your holy hill?
> He whose walk is blameless
> and who does what is righteous,
> who **speaks the truth from his heart...**
> (Psalm 15:1-2 emphasis mine)

Surely you desire **truth in the inner parts**;
    ...you teach me wisdom in the inmost place
(Psalm 51:6 emphasis mine).

The LORD is near to all who call on him,
    ...to all who **call on him in truth** (Psalm
145:18 emphasis mine).

Let's take a look at the story of the woman at the well in
John 4.

Jesus had to make his way to Galilee, and he went
through Samaria to get there. Arriving in Samaria, He
needed a lunch break. He sent the disciples to get lunch,
and then went to the well to get some water. There was a
woman there and He asked her for some water. As she
was drawing from the well, they had a conversation.
Within this conversation is one of the most important
factors in finding deliverance.

After the initial introductions, Jesus moved immediately
into a conversation about water. He told her that He is
the Living Water and that she should be asking Him for a
drink of that water rather than quibbling about whether a
Jew should get water from a Samaritan. As soon as she
heard Him say it, she asked for His Living Water.

Up until then, this was a conversation between two
people talking about a God they both knew a little bit
about, at least as far as the woman knew. But when she
met His challenge to ask for a drink of the Living Water,
Jesus stepped it up a few notches. The first thing He
asked her to do is to go get her husband. Now the reality
of her life came spilling out. Jesus went on to tell her
she'd had several husbands and she was now living with
a man who was not her husband. Here Jesus told the
Samaritan woman the truth and her response to what He
says is very important.

First, look at what Jesus told her. It is clear that He told her something about her life that He had no way of knowing (again, as far as she knew). This action on his part is what we would call a prophecy or a word of knowledge. In other words, he told her something he could only have known because of supernatural knowledge. We know this is true, because even the woman says it is true. See verse 19: "Sir, I can see that you are a prophet."

Once Jesus laid this truth on her, it became her responsibility to decide how she would respond to what he said. As soon as the cat was out of the bag she could have denied it, she could have lied, she could have gotten angry. Think about it for a minute. What is your typical response when someone tells you the truth about yourself?

The story of David and Bathsheba is found in 2 Samuel, chapters 11-12. In chapter 12:1-13, we find the end of a long story that began with David having an affair with Bathsheba, a married woman. When she becomes pregnant, David has her husband murdered.

David goes on with his life effectively unchanged after performing this great sin. Finally Nathan, a prophet, comes to him and tells him a story about a shepherd and a rich man. The rich man has stolen the poor shepherd's prize ewe. David is outraged at the treatment given to the shepherd by the rich man and demands the rich man's life in repayment for the wrong he has done.

The prophet then announces that David is the rich man and Bathsheba the sheep that was stolen. Nathan tells David that the Lord knows of his sin and will punish him.

At this point, David had a number of choices as to how he could react to what Nathan had announced. He could have been angry. He could have lied. He could have blamed someone else. He could have done any number of things to deny the truth of what he had done, but he didn't. When he heard the truth, he faced it and took responsibility for what he had done. David's sin cost him the life of the son born to him by Bathsheba, and he suffered because of this sin several years later. However, because he received and admitted the truth about himself, and then repented, the Lord spared his life and forgave his sin.

Think about how David's story ends if he doesn't choose to tell the truth. What if he chose to blame his sin on his father? What if he chose to blame his sin on Bathsheba? What if he chose blame his sin on Saul? How would that have affected the outcome of David's life?

When you are confronted with your sin, what are the choices you make? Will you choose to become angry with whoever has confronted you? Will you choose to charge them with not knowing enough about what you have been through? Will you accuse them of not having the right to speak the truth?

Is the fact that you are upset proof that you are right?

Does the fact that they don't know intimate details about your life mean that they are wrong?

If you choose to blame someone else for your actions, your choices, your problems, does that actually help you?

I have a hard time believing that these attitudes, thoughts and actions help us. I think we can all recognize that these kinds of defenses only keep the Lord from doing the work that He came to earth to do: that is, to set us free from the kind of entanglements that keep us from having a deeper relationship with Him, that keep us from fulfilling the plans and the ministries the Lord has for us. These defenses perpetuate our problems, and sometimes they even make our problems worse.

We have to become willing to accept the truth about ourselves, our actions and our problems if we are to have any hope of finding the freedom that Christ shed His blood to provide for us.

There are people reading this book who have experienced great troubles in their lives. Some have suffered child abuse, rape, physical assault and many have experienced other horrors too terrible to describe.

Whatever you have suffered in your life may very well not have been your fault. In other words, it *was* not, it *is* not, your fault that you have suffered so. But, your actions and your choices are your responsibility.

An example of this from my own life may help explain what I mean. When I was in my 20s I lived about 250 miles from my parents. One day I was driving along minding my own business when I was pulled over by a police officer. He upheld the law and wrote me a very expensive speeding ticket that I couldn't afford.

The next morning I was cleaning off my windshield from a light snow. I was thinking about my speeding ticket and I became very angry with my parents. Somehow, I had determined that it was their fault that I got a speeding ticket and that I didn't have any money to pay for it.

If I was talking to you about my problem and that I blamed my parents for it, what would you think? Would you agree with me that it was their fault that I got a speeding ticket? I hope not. My parents were at least 250 miles away from my car when I got the ticket. They were completely unaware that I had been speeding and that I had gotten a ticket. Further, unless they were actually in the car holding a gun to my head making me speed, there is no way that it could be their fault that I was speeding. Even though my childhood was somewhat difficult, there was no way I could legitimately or logically blame them for this problem. If I had continued to blame my parents for my speeding ticket and my friends understood me, would that be the best outcome?

Let's say you and I are at a party one evening where we are introduced to Larry. During the party Larry said something that offended me. On our way home I talk to you about what he said. You share with me that it seems as though Larry still carries around some anger about losing his father when he was a little boy. You and I now both have enough knowledge about Larry to understand him a little bit, and we're able to give him some room because of it.

We know that Larry has had a bad experience. We understand him better now than we did before. The problem for Larry is that all the understanding we have for him and why he acts the way he acts is useless for helping him. We have to admit that understanding alone doesn't solve Larry's problems.

As believers, we know that God does something better for us than just understanding our pain. Jesus Christ has already implemented the Father's plan for our healing, recovery and restoration. We also know, as believers, that the way to participate in God's plan is through confession, repentance and forgiveness. When we take responsibility for our words and our actions within this plan we find more than understanding. We find freedom and peace and joy and love. We find freedom from the traps and snares that have entangled us.

Recognizing why you do something and understanding the problem is not the solution in and of itself. It is only the first step. What you do once you have understanding is what determines the outcome. And if your next step is to recognize and embrace the truth about yourself and your thoughts and your actions, then you will start on the path that brings you to full restoration.

What you have to see and agree with and work into your hearts is this: If it's the truth that sets you free, you have to be willing to hear it, no matter how much it hurts. Every time you take responsibility for the thoughts and actions that keep you entrapped, you find freedom. Even when it hurts to do it, when you agree with the truth, then you can find freedom. And restoration.

Remember, we are not talking about weird spiritual stuff here. We aren't talking about something that requires deep spiritual maturity or even a great deal of spiritual power. We are talking about real life and what it takes to find victory. The hardest part about it is that sometimes telling ourselves the truth does not seem like victory. Frequently, it is painful to tell ourselves the truth. But when we go to the Lord and tell Him that we are the ones who made the decision to do this or think that, then we can repent.

Once we have gone to the Lord in this kind of truth He says that He is faithful and just to forgive us and cleanse us from all unrighteousness (I John 1:9).

It's this Word of God's unfailing forgiveness that is our most important weapon. Repentance and cleansing by the blood of Christ is ultimately so important because it sets us free from the guilt and shame the enemy wants to hold over you. This is the objective of the trap. The guilt and shame you feel when we're caught in the enemy's traps is a part of a vicious cycle. You do something that makes you feel bad and then you hurt others. Then you feel worse, and you hurt others again, leading you to feel even more awful.

The only way to end the vicious cycle is to accept the truth and repent of the actions you have taken that led you into the cycle to begin with. Surrendering to God is what is required of you to establish your victory and end the cycle.

This is what it means to die to your self. You recognize that what is holding you in the trap is your fierce grasp on your pain and what caused it. Then you go to God and you tell him the truth. You've been holding on to something that is hurting you. You repent. And then you find your way out of the trap.

Without death there can be no resurrection.

> If we have been united with him like this in his death, we will certainly also be united with him in his resurrection. For we know that our old self was crucified with him so that the body of sin might be done away with, that we should no longer be slaves to sin— because anyone who has died has been freed from sin.
> Now if we died with Christ, we believe that we will also live with him. (Romans 6:5-8)

If your life is in turmoil, take a close look. What is your part? Are you still angry with someone? Do you keep referring to the same event as the cause for your troubles over and over again? It is your burden to come to the Lord and die to the pain they have caused you. You bear the responsibility for who you have become since this terrible thing happened in your life. If you want freedom, if you want to live the resurrection life that is promised to you, the only way you can do it is to die with Christ through repentance so that you may be resurrected into the life and the freedom He has purchased for you.

Some of you may have built your lives around the pain. Many of your friends can understand why you are in pain, and they may be gracious with you. But God has a better plan, a perfect plan for your complete healing and restoration.

If you continue to be in pain over the same thing, you are living what I call the Near-Death Experience. Instead of dying, instead of letting go, you are hanging on to the pain and barely able to survive. It is time now to die to the cause of that pain. Take it to the cross, whatever the pain is, whoever caused it.

The process of dying to yourself is simple to understand, but it can be difficult to work out. No matter how hard it is to work out, it always starts with your choice to take responsibility for your actions and decisions about your life. As soon as you make that choice, you will be on your way out of the Near-Death Experience and on your way to the Resurrection Life.

If you have a hard time grasping this, ask yourself a couple of questions. Is Christ still on the cross? If you agree with me and the Word that He is not on the cross, then where is He? Is He still suffering? Does He still hurt? Is He in pain? The answer to these questions is that He is in heaven and He is not on the cross and He is not in pain. Everything He did for you He did one time, for all.

The enemy has held you in a trap and built a stronghold around you. It will take a battle to get free. You can begin that battle now. Some of you are going to walk through a short intense battle and others will go through a longer battle. Up until now, you haven't been under attack as much as you have been trapped, unable to get free from your fears and pains.

Christ has secured your victory. It is time for you to join the battle to gain your freedom. The cost of joining the battle is to hear, speak and agree with the truth. Tell the Lord that you are ready to listen and hear the truth. Then act according to what you know you should do because of that truth.

Chapter 5

How Does God See You?

Many of the books we read and movies we see at the theater or on television are stories of love gone wrong. The beautiful, wonderful and powerful thing we call love somehow turns into a weapon used by one character in the story to hurt another. In one story the weapon might be heard in a statement like this: "If you loved me, you would…" In a different story we might hear, "I don't love you anymore. You're not who I thought you were." When love, given or withdrawn, is based on some kind of performance, it can drive us to do terrible things.

Love, or at least so-called love, has brought ruin to many lives. Some mothers have hurt children by withdrawing love for messy rooms or other offenses. On the other hand, some mothers have changed their children's lives by successfully communicating their love for their children unconditionally. Fathers have done the same. Look at the major characters of the Bible. Jacob loved Joseph more than all his children (Genesis 37:3). David loved Solomon not Adonijah (1 Kings 1:13). The giving and taking of love has surprising impact on people's lives. Psychological studies have shown that even the appearance, or the illusion, of love has a positive impact on rhesus monkey babies. Rhesus monkey babies who received love even appear to live better lives, are more socially accepted and have higher rankings in their clans than those who were deprived of a mother's love. (See http://www.livescience.com/culture/090206-hn-baby-chimps.html).

We shouldn't be surprised to find that love can be a

spiritual weapon. Paul talks about this to the Ephesians in verses 3:14-19. The positive, encouraging and continual application of the love of God, by God, to our lives works good within us, surpassing our understanding to produce the fruits of the Spirit we all seek. The negative, discouraging and continual disruption of God's love by the enemy works destruction within us in the same way.

For us, the question becomes how should we understand love so that its use as a weapon against us is disarmed? And how does love in our favor become a dangerous weapon of warfare for the kingdom of God? We need to learn how God sees us, how He loves us, in order to find the strength and resources to fight for our personal deliverance.

If we are honest with ourselves we have to say that we need to know this love of God as soon as possible. We need to know His love in a way we can grasp right now. We need this "right now" because the battles some of us are facing are very fierce and painful. And we really do ask sometimes, "Why God? Why?" And the real, tangible, right here and now answer has to be that we know that God loves us.

Take a minute to reflect on the following two questions. First, do you know that God loves you? Second, do you know God's love? It may seem, at first, that these two questions are the same. But, they're not. The answer to the first question will come from what you know the Bible says about God and His love for you. The answer to the second question will come from what you know in your heart about God and his love for you.

One of the reasons the enemy has so much success is that he is very good at making us doubt that God loves us. For instance, if I ask you how God feels about you when you sin, I suspect that most of you would say He is mad at you. It's like we have this picture of Him standing in heaven with His arms crossed, looking down at us and shaking His head in disapproval at every little thing we do that is wrong. However it happened, we have come to believe that God is constantly angry with us.

This picture we have of God is in direct contrast with what the Word says about Him. God wants you to know more about Him and how he loves you than you do right now, and we are going to find out about that as we examine the scripture.

God's love for us is revealed in Jesus Christ. Think about everything Jesus did when He was here on earth. The first thing you see is that every healing, every deliverance, every work of power was about love, not power. And every work of love expressed in His power was an act of spiritual warfare.

See Ephesians 3:16-21 and look at how Paul talks about power and love together.

> I pray that out of his glorious riches he may strengthen you with power through his Spirit in your inner being, so that Christ may dwell in your hearts through faith. And I pray that you, being rooted and established in love, may have power, together with all the saints, to grasp how wide and long and high and deep is the love of Christ, and to know this love that surpasses knowledge–that you may be filled to the measure of all the fullness of God. Now to him who is able to do immeasurably more than all we ask or imagine, according to his power that is at work within us, to him be glory in the church and in Christ Jesus throughout all generations, for ever and ever! Amen (Ephesians 3:17-21).

Notice that the objective of Paul's prayer is that we would receive power for one purpose: To grasp the love of Christ!

To find out more about this love we need to look at it differently than we have before. We need to see how Christ loves us so that we can know how he wants us to love others and to love ourselves. I think the best way to do this is to look at what Christ called the greatest commandments:

> "Teacher, which is the greatest commandment in the Law?" Jesus replied: "'Love the Lord your God with all your heart and with all your soul and with all your mind.' This is the first and greatest commandment. And the second is like it: 'Love your neighbor as yourself.' All the Law and the Prophets hang on these two commandments (Matthew 22:36-40).

Jesus said that the greatest commandment is to love the Lord your God with all of your heart … and the other, which is like it, is this: To love your neighbor as yourself. There are three tasks assigned to us here:

- Love God
- Love others
- Love yourself

I think what happens to us as we fight for our personal deliverance is that the enemy tells us God doesn't really love us because we aren't good enough or because we aren't any good at loving others. If we believe what he tells us, it becomes difficult to love God. This is because if we don't believe that God loves us, then we must find our own resource, our own capacity to love others. And when we fail at both, it becomes difficult to love anyone, let alone ourselves.

When we change our thoughts and feelings about God and His love for us, we will be much more successful at finding our personal deliverance. As we teach our hearts that God really does love us, we can begin to believe that he does not base His love on our performance. Rather, our Father loves us in spite of our performance because His Son demonstrated the perfect performance on our behalf. Look at what John says about this:

> This is how God showed his love among us: He sent his one and only Son into the world that we might live through him (1 John 4:9).

We know God loves us. The Bible tells us so. But many of us don't know how He loves us. We don't know how He sees us…we don't know the action He takes or the attitude He takes toward us because of His love for us. To make an informed and righteous decision to change our thoughts and feelings about how God loves us we must determine how He loves us, how He sees us. We will base our determination on I Corinthians 13. This chapter of the Bible is recognized by people who are unbelievers as one of the great definitions of love. If we can grasp Paul's definition of love we may be able to begin to apply it to our own lives and the lives of others.

> Love is patient, love is kind. It does not envy, it does not boast, it is not proud. It is not rude, it is not self-seeking, it is not easily angered, it keeps no record of wrongs. Love does not delight in evil but rejoices with the truth. It always protects, always trusts, always hopes, always perseveres. Love never fails…(1 Corinthians 13:4-8).

Our effort to grasp this definition of love will be rewarded with the answer to one simple question: How does God love us? If we can answer this one question we will be able to understand how we are supposed to love both others and ourselves.

John confirms that we should know this love:

> And so we know and rely on the love God has for us. **God is love.** Whoever lives in love lives in God, and God in him (1 John 4:16 emphasis mine).

We can see from these three passages that Jesus, Paul and John placed a great emphasis on love. John said that God is love. Paul defined love and Jesus said that love is the keyword, or foundation, of the greatest commandments.

In order to understand the primary message of thinking about the love of God for us in the context of 1 Corinthians 13, let's go back to I John 4.

> Dear friends, let us love one another, for love comes from God. Everyone who loves has been born of God and knows God. Whoever does not love does not know God, because God is love …. We love because he first loved us (1 John 4:7-8, 19).

In I John 4 we find that God is love and that we love because He first loved us. This answers the question, "Why should we love God?" by giving the answer, "Because He first loved us." As we love God we live in obedience to what Christ said was the greatest commandment. The next logical question should be, "How do we know that God loves us?" Look at 1 John 4:9-10.

> This is how God showed his love among us: He sent his one and only Son into the world that we

might live through him. This is love: not that we loved God, but that he loved us and sent his Son as an atoning sacrifice for our sins (1 John 4:9-10).

John is right, of course. God gave His only Son so that we could "live through him." Yet many of us continue to think of God's love as a concept and not a reality. We continue to think that He is always harsh with us, lacking understanding of our circumstances and withholding grace and mercy. Yet the Word directly refutes this idea (see Hebrews 4:15-16). This is why we are so ready to believe that God is out to punish us. However, Paul and John prove that this isn't true. God is not asking us to be patient and slow to anger and continually hopeful while He is standing at the ready to punish us over and over again.

Most of us already know that God sent His Son to become an atoning sacrifice. He sent His Son for our salvation because He loves us. He loved us then, He loves us now and He will always love us. What we don't know in a practical, present or "right now" manner is how He actually loves us. That's where I Corinthians 13 comes in. As beautiful and poetic as this passage is, it is every bit practical and "right now."

Take a closer look at some of the traits Paul uses to describe love and recall that John stated that God is love. Love:

- Is slow to anger
- Is patient
- Is kind
- Keeps no record of wrongs
- Trusts
- Hopes
- Never fails

So, if God is love and love is slow to anger, then God is slow to anger. If love is patient, then God is patient. If God is love and love is kind and trusting and hoping for your best, then God is kind and trusting and hoping for your best. God keeps no record of your wrongs. God and His love never fail.

So, not only has God sent His Son to be an atonement for us, to redeem us and claim us as His own, as His possession, He also really, beautifully and practically loves us right now and forever.

I look at what Jesus said and what John and Paul wrote about love in these passages as being interrelated. Taken together as we have just viewed them, we can see answers to questions that may have been difficult for us to put together before. We love because He first loved us. Our questions about His love are answered with two proofs. We can see in the Gospels God's sacrifice of His Son for our salvation. We can see in 1 Corinthians 13 the traits of love that describe how He loves us.

Seeing these two proofs and understanding the **concept** of His love isn't sufficient to change our lives. As a body of believers we have, for too long, readily accepted that God is always standing at the ready to punish us. This belief has tainted everything in our walk with God.

Apply John's statement that God is love and Paul's description of love to answer the question, "How does God love us?" As you think about the answer to this question, what will the impact of God's love be in your heart? Will you now be able to apply His love in your life in places you've previously been unable to?

The difficulty we face, as human beings and as a church, is that we learn ways that seem to bypass our ability to discern the truth. So, when we sin and then we encounter a real or imagined consequence to our sin we imagine that God is punishing us.

Here's an example of what I mean. Over the last few years I tried my hand at making a living in sales. I encountered very little success. In the middle of my attempt to find success in this new career I began to have trouble with sin. I fell into a sin that I hadn't had any trouble with for years. As I was struggling, I was making a connection in my mind between my sin and my lack of success in sales. I began to think that God was punishing me.

As I was thinking this idea through, it occurred to me that I missed something when I drew this conclusion. The truth was that I had experienced little to no success for some time before I began to struggle with this sin. If that was true, then it couldn't be that God was punishing me for my sin. My lack of success may have had something to do with me, but whatever the difficulty was, it wasn't that God was punishing me. It's not that I make light of my sin. The problem with persisting in sin is that we continually choose something other than a deep relationship with the Lord. In addition, persisting in sin gives the enemy an opportunity to exploit our weaknesses and catch us in one of those traps. Whatever trouble I was having wasn't due to God's punishment for my failings. I had to change my understanding about the circumstance I was in.

In fact, I had discovered quite a bit of unbelief in my heart and asked the Holy Spirit to reveal it to me so I could replace it with belief. The Holy Spirit was showing me my own lack of belief in God's love for me. As I began to understand this, I took the steps we have talked about. I told the truth about myself and I repented of two sins. I repented of the sin I was struggling with that was easy to see. I also repented of the other sin that the Spirit showed me. I repented of my unbelief. The joyful conclusion to the story is that I have been free from this sin for some time now. And I have found a deeper belief in His love for me. God hasn't rejected me. I am beginning to understand how much He has done to truly accept me.

The Bible has a lot more to say about God's love for you than it does about His punishment. It seems as though many of us attribute the bad things that happen in our lives as though God was punishing us, while we seem very reluctant to believe that He loves us. This is what the enemy wants in his fight against us. He wants us to believe that God doesn't really even like us. But everywhere we turn in scripture we find that God loves us, is patient with us, hopes for us and is slow to anger with us.

If you were to imagine what it would be like to be truly loved and if you could write down everything that would make you feel that way, God's love would so far exceed what you had written down it would be impossible for you to compare. This is the point of Paul's prayer in Ephesians 3. Paul is praying that you would know how wide and long and high and deep God's love is for you. And then He says God is able to do immeasurably more than you could ask or think, so that you know his prayer for you will be answered. God's love for you is perfect. His love for you is eternal. His love for you is dependable.

It's knowing God's love that makes it possible for you to face your battles with confidence. God supplies you with the love, joy and peace to walk through the battles you face. It's knowing His love for you that gives you the strength to overcome and the power to be thankful, the desire to worship and the ability to honor and forgive the people in your life.

Chapter 6

Choosing Thankfulness

The most important decision we have ever made is the decision to receive the salvation God has offered us through the death and resurrection of Jesus Christ. For many, the first experience with Christ illustrates His power to release us from the traps and the snares the enemy has caught us in. At the same time, many of us have not fully experienced God's salvation in our lives. There may be many good reasons for this. One of the most overlooked reasons for missing out on the fullness of God's salvation is that we have not become thankful people.

I want to propose to you that there is a difference between **being** more thankful and **becoming** more thankful.

It's not that I'm looking at you with my hands on my hips, wagging my finger at you saying you should be more thankful.

This is a different message. The message is that we all are able to make a decision to become more thankful. Here's the distinction between the two.

When I stand with my hands on my hips, wagging my finger at you, I am telling you to behave better, to act more thankful. Instead, the message I want to convey is that we should desire to *become* more thankful. Being more thankful is an outward action generated for the sake of a performance. It is an act rather than an attitude. The act is not without value, but it is without perseverance or persistence and it may not be part of our character. When there is no one around to see the performance of the act of thankfulness, the performance ceases.

The decision to *become* more thankful is a decision to make an inward change of heart. This is more valuable because it results both in being more thankful and becoming more thankful. Thankfulness will become part of your character even when there is no one around to see the activity or watch you work it out.

There must be a good scriptural basis for making the effort to change something inside of us. It is hard enough to act thankful when people are watching, let alone when we are by ourselves. Sometimes the simplest things to understand are the most difficult to work out. Why should we work so hard on this one simple thing?

David understood the importance of being thankful. He wrote what God has to say about giving thanks in difficult times in Psalm 50.

Here is Psalm 50:23 from several translations of Scripture:

> NIV He who sacrifices thank offerings honors me, and he prepares the way so that I may show him the salvation of God.
>
> KJV Whoso offereth praise glorifieth me: and to him that ordereth his conversation aright will I shew the salvation of God.
>
> NLT But giving thanks is a sacrifice that truly honors me. If you keep to my path, I will reveal to you the salvation of God.

What does the word salvation mean? Many seem to think that salvation is kind of like a movie ticket. It's like I made a date with Jesus to go to a movie. We planned to meet at the theater just before the show starts. Before the "date" I go about my life as I normally would. There's no need for any interaction before the movie because I have other things to do and I know I will see Him later. Not only that, but in this scenario Jesus has the same attitude. He knows I have the ticket and He will see me later, but between now and then there really is no need to communicate or be involved. Our date will occur sometime in the future and when it does, it will be great, but until then, what's the point of getting together?

I don't think this is what God the Father had in mind when He sacrificed His Son and then exerted His power in Him to raise Him from the dead. I think what He has in mind is something more immediate, something more present, something more right now! We don't have to wait for heaven to experience salvation in its truest meaning. The intention has always been that we would experience it yesterday, today and tomorrow. In fact, when we look at the meaning of the word salvation we find that it has a meaning we haven't fully realized.

The word for salvation in Hebrew is *yesha* (pronounced yay-shah; Strong's Exhaustive Concordance #H3468).

Yesha means this: **deliverance, salvation, rescue, safety, welfare.**

> a. safety, welfare, prosperity
> b. salvation
> c. victory

Wouldn't it be wonderful to have this salvation actively working in your life *every day?* It can. Look at the instruction given in Psalm 50:23. The New International Version instructs us to sacrifice thank offerings. The King James says that we should order our conversation aright, and the New Living Translation again talks about giving thanks as a sacrifice. How do we do this in a day when there is no "act," such as an animal sacrifice, to perform? We sacrifice thank offerings by determining with an active choice of our will to become thankful, even when it seems we should be ungrateful. We choose. We decide with purpose to become thankful even in a troubling circumstance. We determine to order our conversation aright by choosing to speak out loud our thankfulness to the Lord.

As believers we know that one of the things we have chosen to do is to honor God. As we offer our thanks we honor Him, and he immediately responds by saying He will do something for us in return.

What is it that He will do for us in return? What is the promise given to us when we act according to the instruction of Psalm 50:23? It is clear from all three versions. God will show us His deliverance, His salvation, His prosperity and His victory.

He will show us His salvation.

I meet people all the time who want to know what God's will is for their life. It's common among believers that we want to know what God wants us to do. Sometimes we are looking for change, and sometimes we want to know how to handle the change that we're in the midst of. We want to know if we should go into the ministry or get married or take a different job or move to another city. Maybe you have been frustrated and confused because you haven't felt like you were hearing from God. The first step toward solving the problem of finding God's will for your life is to decide to become a thankful person.

1 Thessalonians 5:18 gives us one of the reasons why we should want to become more thankful as children of God:

> Be joyful always; pray continually; **give thanks in all circumstances, for this is God's will for you in Christ Jesus** (emphasis mine).

If you want to know God's will for your life, it's right here. Look at verse 18: "this is God's will for you."

Do you get caught up in your need to hear from God while you're still unwilling to do the simplest thing He has asked you to do? Do you become frustrated when one of your friends, hearing your situation, says, "Work on being more thankful?"

You're not alone. All of us have big questions for God. We want to know if we should be missionaries or pastors, accountants or teachers. We want to know which girl or boy we should marry. We want our friends to give us a word from God to tell us exactly what to do. We want a word from God tailored to our circumstance. We want to know the deeper thing, the idea or clue that will suddenly clear everything up for us. One of the most important, and often overlooked, clues to the answers for your big questions is this one: Determine in your heart to become a thankful person.

I can think of at least one more reason to become thankful. Wouldn't it be glorious to spend our days in the courtyards of the King? Of course, it would, but how do we do that?

One of the answers to this question can found in Psalm 100:

Enter into his gates with thanksgiving, and into his courts with praise: be thankful unto him, and bless his name (Psalm 100:4).

As we focus on verse 4 we learn a simple instruction about how we can spend more time in the presence of the Lord

Some of us have heard this psalm as a song before. In college, I used to play my guitar and sing it. It's too bad that when I put my guitar down and went back to class that I immediately forgot its message. I've spent most of my Christian life thinking that it's difficult to get close to God. Somehow I misunderstood the requirements. I thought that getting close to God required me to fast and to be an evangelist and to do things that are too far from what I know I can do. The message in Psalm 100 is different. Its message is that I can enter His presence simply by being thankful and blessing his name. David puts this clear message in a song that's easy to sing and to remember: "Enter His gates with thanksgiving and into His courts with praise..."

A few years ago we took my oldest son to California to attend a small university in Costa Mesa. We stayed in a hotel across the street from Disneyland. I managed to find a way not to have to go to the park with everyone else (I'm not a fan of big amusement parks), but I walked all over the courtyards when we were there. The night before everyone went into the park we all went to a restaurant and shopped at the stores in its courtyards. We watched street musicians play different kinds of music, and we enjoyed the Wonderful World of Disney. If you have ever been to one of these kinds of places you know a little bit about being in the courtyards of heaven. At Disneyland, the courtyards were peaceful and relaxing. They were full of life, and people were happy. And there was no entry fee to get into the courtyard. The "cost" of admission was decent behavior, and you could stay in the courtyard as long as it was open.

The entry fee, the ticket, to the courtyards of God's throne room is simply your expression of thankfulness to God. The length of time you stay in the courtyard of the King is dependent on your perseverance in becoming thankful. Enter the courtyard by beginning to express your thankfulness. If you have ever wondered what you can **do** to draw near to the Lord, then this is one of the answers you have been looking for. The Lord will always receive your thanksgiving. It is impossible to be displeasing to Him when you are expressing thanksgiving to Him. Practice the act of thankfulness over and over and it will begin to become part of your nature and your character. Thankfulness will become a trait people use to describe you. In fact, when you remain thankful in a difficult time it is a testimony to the work God has done in your life. People can see peace in you that can only come from having a deeper walk with God. People are able to see the simplicity with which you approach life. In every circumstance you are able to identify those things that you are thankful for.

Jesus, David and Paul all had more things to say about thankfulness. Look at the story of the 10 lepers in Luke 17:11-19. In this story Jesus was only really impressed with the one leper who returned to give Him thanks. Jesus told him that his faith had made him well.

David said, "It is a good thing to give thanks unto the Lord…" in Psalm 92:1 (KJV). And Paul talks about thankfulness again in Philippians:

> Rejoice in the Lord always. I will say it again: Rejoice! Let your gentleness be evident to all. The Lord is near. Do not be anxious about anything, but in everything, by prayer and petition, with

thanksgiving, present your requests to God. And the peace of God, which transcends all understanding, will guard your hearts and your minds in Christ Jesus (Philippians 4:4-7).

Paul's instruction to us is simple. Tell the Lord everything: all of your needs and wants. Look closely, though, and you'll see that Paul is also telling you how to place your needs and wants in the context of thankfulness. Here's what he's getting at. As you come before the Lord to let Him know about your life, begin by telling God that you are thankful. As in one of the examples above, you might thank him for your family or your job. As you thank God for your family or your job, tell him the things you see as needs and wants:

> "Thank you for my job, Lord. You have made a good provision for me in this job. I would like to be more challenged, take on greater responsibility. Again, I thank you for what you have given me. You put me in a place where I have been able to grow. I believe I am ready for the next step. Will You lead me on the right path, so I can take that next step? Thank You, Lord."

See how this prayer places your needs and wants in the context of thanksgiving? This is what Paul is driving at. This is what he is teaching the Philippians to do.

I have three children. I have lived through the trials and tribulations of having my children grow through their teenage years. My third child is about to begin the journey. When they were teenagers, the two older children were just like all the other teenagers in the world: It was amazing how sweet they could be when they wanted something. They gave me smiles and the happy faces and the seemingly good attitudes. My oldest son, in particular, was pretty good at "working it" before he left for college. My daughter has learned how to "work it," too. When they come to ask me for something and they are happy and make me laugh, it is always more likely that I will give them the answer they're looking for. When they ask for things with expressions of disgust and disdain, or when they react poorly to rules their mother and I enforce, I become less likely to give them what they want.

Of course, God isn't as easily manipulated as me. He isn't manipulated at all. Yet, the instructions are clear, and the examples of what happens when His people aren't grateful abound. See what happened to the children of Israel when they were wandering in the desert. Rather than being thankful and presenting God with their needs for water and shelter and food, they complained bitterly. Their complaints and bitterness fostered a poor relationship with God. A whole generation wandered in the desert and never saw the Promised Land. God wants us to be thankful for what He gives us and where He leads us. He said He will show us His salvation when we choose to be thankful. When we are thankful, we effectively release Him to work His will out in our life. And we may well find ourselves with another opportunity to exercise the thankfulness that has become a part of our nature.

The greatest challenges most of us have in our walk with the Lord have to do with how we'll respond to teaching and preaching. The first decision we face when we read or hear a message is whether we will act on it. Will we say, "I can do this, I want to do this."

This message is simple and clear: Choose to become a thankful person. Express thanksgiving to God even when it seems like you should be ungrateful. You should do this because you're hungry for more of God's salvation in your life. Tell your heart this is what you want. Say to yourself, "I can do this!"

To activate this weapon called "thanksgiving," you have to actually say in your heart and with your mouth that you are thankful. Not just once or twice but over and over again. Imagine the epitaph on your tombstone. Could it say, "He or she was the most thankful person we ever knew." What would it take for that to happen for you?

Maybe you're asking the question, "How can I be thankful in my circumstance?" Maybe it's difficult to find something to be thankful for. But God is ready to help. Psalm 25 speaks to God's readiness to help us learn His ways:

> Show me your ways, O LORD,
>   teach me your paths;
> guide me in your truth and teach me,
>   for you are God my Savior,
>   and my hope is in you all day long.
>
> Good and upright is the LORD;
>   therefore he instructs sinners in his ways.
> He guides the humble in what is right
>   and teaches them his way.
> All the ways of the LORD are loving and faithful
>   for those who keep the demands of his
>   covenant (Psalm 25:4-5, 8-10).

You can see here that God never wanted to leave us alone to our own troubles and wait for us to work them out. He has always wanted to teach you His ways. He has always wanted to rescue you. The trouble is that by your words and by your actions you rarely allow Him the opportunity to work His salvation out in your life. It's easy to be ignorant of our need to be thankful, especially when things are going well. Yet the simplest thing you can choose to do is to become thankful and begin to express thanks to Him even in the midst of oppressing trials and tribulations. Upon receiving Christ as our Savior, the single most important thing you can do is to purpose to become thankful for what God has provided you.

Jesus confirms what the psalmist says when He tells the disciples about the Holy Spirit in John 14.

> But the Counselor, the Holy Spirit, whom the Father will send in my name, will teach you all things and will remind you of everything I have said to you (John 14:26).

When you decide to become a thankful person, you have to start from where you are. Here are a couple of quick tips from what I have learned about becoming thankful:

1) Begin thanking God for everything. I read a book a long time ago that talked about being thankful. The author of the book said that he started thanking God for things like light bulbs and trees and sun and shade. Why? Because he took so much for granted that he forgot the blessings that were right there in front of him.

2) The second tip I have for you is this: Ask the Holy Spirit to help you. Jesus said that He would send the Holy Spirit to guide you into all truth (John 16:13).

I learned both of these 'tips' through the same experience. I was talking with my wife one day about her mother, Emma Lou. Emma Lou used to tell Donna things about the boys Donna dated. I was really enjoying the conversation. It was wonderful to know all about all the

81

boys my wife dated before me. I have friends who are pretty sure I "out-kicked my coverage," when I married her. So, it was nice to know that the other boys who dated Donna weren't all that hot according to her mother!

Donna talked about a warning her mother had given her about one boy she dated. Emma Lou told her he wasn't a thankful person. I was so struck by that statement that I thought it needed additional attention. That is when I bought a book about thankfulness. I began to follow its instruction, and I kept a journal of some of my experiences at the time. I really put effort into the decision to become more thankful.

I could sense that I was making progress. Then I got fired from my job as an assistant manager at a video store. At the time my oldest son was a three-year-old toddler and my wife was pregnant with our second child. You can imagine that it was a difficult time. I was able to find peace, though, when I was at home alone one morning not long after I was fired. I was walking around my living room asking the Lord about my situation. I had recently come to understand that much of my circumstance in having difficulty keeping a job had nothing to do with needing deliverance or being "under attack." It had more to do with the fact that I frequently acted like a jerk. I thought I knew everything, and I wasn't afraid to tell everyone about it. I was ungrateful, and I was stuck in a trap of the enemy's making.

As I walked around my house, I said to the Lord, "I know I act like a jerk most of the time, but there are a lot of jerks out there who can keep their jobs and make money. How am I supposed to be thankful in this situation?" I heard the Lord ask me a question. He said, "Tell me about the families of the jerks you are thinking about." I thought about it for a minute, and I concluded that most of the people I was thinking about had miserable lives

82

outside of work. They had families in disarray and children in trouble. The list of their troubles went on and on. I learned that I could give the Lord thanks for the wonderful family He gave me.

I didn't understand at the time that I was talking with the Holy Spirit. I have learned to develop a relationship with the Holy Spirit since this experience. As we saw above, Jesus sent the Holy Spirit to teach us. Teachers love questions. They love to ask questions and they love to answer questions. These days, when I encounter a situation or an idea I'm not sure about I simply ask the Holy Spirit questions. Asking, "How am I supposed to be thankful in this situation?" is an example of praying and asking for an answer that God wants to give.

When I asked my question, "How can I be thankful?" The Holy Spirit's response directed me to be thankful for what I have. I understood that I could be thankful in this situation because I had a wonderful family. And so I walked around for about six more weeks focusing on the practice of being thankful for what the Lord had told me to be thankful for. I said out loud, "Lord, thank you for my family," and "Thank you for helping me find a job." I continued in thankfulness on a daily basis. Every time I thought about my circumstance and became angry or afraid I would stop. I would repeat my thankfulness to the Lord. At the time I really didn't know what else to do. I had come to a place in my life where, in spite of all the books I read and the Bible verses I knew, I was incapable of any spiritual understanding. As I talked about earlier I was a very immature believer at the time. My spirit was underdeveloped and my brain was over developed. When I recognized this problem, I stopped everything I was doing to overcome my circumstance and looked for one instruction I could understand. The only verse in the Bible I could read and understand at the time was 1

Thessalonians 5:18, "in everything give thanks, for this is the will of God for you."

Shortly after this time spent with the Lord, a woman from our church told Donna that an insurance company was hiring. While the jobs they would be hiring for had little to do with the degrees I had obtained in college, I had nothing to lose and everything to gain by applying for work there. I was relieved and surprised to be hired, since at the time I lacked not only experience, but also self-confidence. I have been working in some capacity within the financial services industry ever since. I have a lot to be thankful for.

Do you want God to come and work His salvation, His power, in the middle of your circumstance?

Prepare the way to the wholeness and reality of God's salvation in the middle of your circumstance as you give Him thanks.

Do you want to know the will of God? You can start by giving Him thanks.

Do you want to be closer to the Lord than you have ever been? Enter His gates with Thanksgiving.

When I determined to become a thankful person, I thought I knew a lot about God. Unfortunately, I didn't know Him very well. When I cried out to the Lord, He sent the Holy Spirit to teach me. Jesus said that His yoke is easy and his burden is light. It wasn't complex to decide to become thankful. It has been hard sometimes, but I get the concept, and I submit to God's requirement. I continue to develop thankfulness within me, because the reward is great. I have seen God's salvation work in my life. I have been delivered from many troubles. I believe much of that deliverance has come from my being willing to be thankful in difficult times.

As you began to get your words right about God and your circumstance, you will find it easier to become thankful. You will become thankful that He loves you like He says He loves you. And you will become thankful that He performs His Word the way He says He performs His Word.

The truth is that if we concentrate on the simple things they will lead us to the deeper things. We want more than we're ready for most of the time. And because this is true, we end up missing what God has for us now. So, if you're looking for God's will in your life as you face a major decision or a difficult circumstance, let me encourage you to practice your thankfulness until thankfulness becomes part of your nature so that you *become* a thankful person.

Chapter 7

Discovering Personal Worship

"You are my God, and I make a covenant with you that you are my God and I will worship you."
                                                                          -Dr. Norvel Hayes

Now we turn to worship in order to learn its place as a weapon of spiritual war. At its simplest level worship (and praise) is telling the truth about God to Him, to us and to our enemies. It is a weapon of war for at least two reasons. Personal worship establishes our connection with God as our teacher, and personal worship is the vehicle through which we establish intimacy with God. As a weapon of war, personal worship of God results in the strengthening of our relationship and bond with the One who protects us and delivers us.

At some point in my walk with God, I began to notice that some of the Christians I know are stronger and more able than others. By able, I mean that they hear from God more clearly, pray more effectively and impact the lives of others more deeply. Observing them, I began to desire a walk with God like they had. I continued to observe these men and women to see if I could find out what was different about them. The common experience they all seem to have in their walk is that they know God. I began to want to know God. For a long time as I worked to get to know God better, I felt as though I was making little progress. I tried to behave better. I tried to serve more. I read a lot of books. I prayed. I fasted. After all my work I found I didn't know God any better than I did when I started. I knew God was there, but I couldn't feel Hi. I couldn't sense Him.

At about this time, I became friends with a missionary family. They had recently moved back to the United States from South Africa and began to attend my church. The husband had been diagnosed with cancer. Soon, the cancer grew bad enough that he could no longer participate in the church choir. I would visit with him every week during choir practice so he wouldn't feel alone.

I was telling some of my friends at work about this man, and it turned out that they knew him. They thought, since we were all Christians, I could somehow pray for him and he would be healed. Apparently, they didn't know that I was a 98-pound weakling in my spirit. One of my friends decided that I should listen to a cassette tape series about healing by a man named Dr. Norvel Hayes. I hadn't listened to tapes for a very long time, and I wasn't very interested in listening to the series. But I decided that I could at least try them for a few minutes before giving them back to my friend if I didn't like what I heard.

It turns out that Dr. Hayes is a man with a good Southern drawl who tells good stories. I found myself looking forward to listening to the tapes. Dr. Hayes said a lot of good things about faith and healing and God. And then he said something that changed my life. He was telling a story about his own life and how worship is so important. He became quite expressive as he said, "If you want to know God, worship God!" He said it three times.

I don't remember anything else about those tapes, but I remember those words. When I heard them, it was like a little bell went off in my head. I said, "I can do that!" I didn't have anything to lose, I thought. I might as well go ahead and worship God. The trouble was that I didn't know how to worship God.

So I began to say, "Praise the Lord, praise the Lord, praise the Lord," over and over again. In the shower when I got up. In the car on the way to work. In the hallways at work when I thought no one could hear me. In bed at night before I went to sleep. I did this for about three days. I was getting worn out. I said to the Lord, "If this is what you want me to do for the rest of my life I will do it because I want to know You. But this has to be completely boring for you. Will you teach me how to worship?"

Over the next few months I began to learn how to worship God. There were revivals happening in various places throughout the nation at the time. I felt the Lord asking me to go to my own church and pray for revival. I didn't know the first thing about praying for revival, but I decided to go to church once a week and pray anyway. The first time I went to the church to pray, I decided that since I didn't know how to pray for revival I would worship God until He showed me what to pray. It turned out to be an intense experience. Even though I didn't know how to pray for revival, the Holy Spirit would help me pray. I felt an intensity in prayer that I had never felt before. Many times, I felt as though the Holy Spirit was telling me what and how to pray. I would pray for about a half hour and then go to work. Every time I went to church to pray I had a similar experience.

One morning I was on the way to church to pray. I was very distracted, thinking about my bills and things that needed repair in my house and with my car. I figured that when I got to church I would be able to pray and then return to my own worries. I arrived at the church and I began to worship, but I was missing the intensity I had experienced with the Holy Spirit.   I decided to get a Bible to look up a verse that would help me. I intended to pray through Ephesians 6, "our battle is not against flesh and blood, but against powers and principalities," but I mixed up my scripture references and went to 2 Corinthians 10:4-5 instead.

> The weapons we fight with are not the weapons of the world. On the contrary, they have divine power to demolish strongholds. We demolish arguments and every pretension that sets itself up against the knowledge of God, and we take captive every thought to make it obedient to Christ (2 Corinthians 10:4-5).

As I read through verse 5 I felt as though I was struck by lightning. I had always thought that the arguments and pretenses Paul was talking about demolishing were those of Buddhists, Hindus and any other religion that is set up against God. But, I was struck by the thought that I have my own arguments and pretenses set up against the knowledge of God. I had a chance to ponder that idea for just about one second before I was struck by lightning again.

If I have arguments and pretenses that are set up against the knowledge of God, it must be that God wants me to know Him!

Well, that just blew me away. I had been a Christian for at least 25 years by then. I had lived through times of nearness to God and times of distance from God. In all that time, I never knew that He wanted me to know Him. Me. But there it is in His Word. He wouldn't go to the trouble of demolishing the arguments and pretenses that I have set up against knowing Him if He didn't want me to know Him. The logic is irrefutable. It was no longer a concept. It became a reality. God wanted and wants me to know Him.

For all my life I felt as though I was one of the scruffy little kids on the outside of the circle around Jesus. I didn't think He would ever look at me and ask me to come near to Him. I was wrong. All along He wanted me to know Him. My life has been changed by this one experience. I am more mature now. I hear God's voice better now. But I wouldn't be here if I hadn't heard God's Word the way I did that morning – and that wouldn't have happened if I hadn't learned about worship.

Of course, this experience made me want to worship Him more. I'm not a great musician or wonderfully talented in any special way, but I am still able to worship the Lord as He has taught me. I still worship Him every chance I get. I make the decision to worship the Lord. Sometimes the decision is easy and sometimes it is more difficult. But, in the same way I have determined to be thankful, I have determined to worship the Lord. When I worship the Lord, I am strengthened in Him and by Him. He is worthy of my praise all the time. He is glorious and wonderful. He is my Counselor. He leads me when I don't know where to go. He cares for me when I am feeling low.

In addition to making a clear point that if we want to know God we have to worship Him, Dr. Hayes frequently makes this statement (from Psalm 118:28): "You are my God, and I make a covenant with you that you are my God and I will worship you." Worship is the vehicle through which we establish a personal connection with God. When you determine to make this covenant with God, you establish that connection.

Chapter 8

Establish Your Worship Connection

Come, let us bow down in worship, let us kneel before the LORD our Maker; for he is our God and we are the people of his pasture, the flock under his care (Psalm 95:6-7).

As I began to talk to my friends and anyone who would listen about my experience with worship, I heard many responses. Chief among the responses were several versions of this statement: "I worship God by doing a good job at work," or "by loving my family." In fact you may be saying the same thing to yourself as you read through this chapter. I think this statement misdirects us in our relationship with God.

It's important that you do a good job at work. It's important that you love your family and give tithes and offerings. These acts and others like them **honor** God. But **worship** is a separate act. It is done with the intent of truly worshipping God and is not something you get to include in your jobs as employees, family members or church attendees. If you are willing to make a covenant with God that He is your God and that you will worship Him, then you must actually worship Him.

Why is it important to establish your connection with God by worshipping Him? Worship is ascribing worth to God. It is derived from a combo word, worth-ship.

When you ascribe "worth-ship" to God you tell Him that you believe He is great, He is worthy of your praise. You tell Him that you are willing to give Him glory for everything He has done.

In Psalm 25:14 we see one of the greatest benefits of worshipping God. The Lord will actually confide in those who fear (or worship) Him.

> The Lord confides in those who fear him; he makes his covenant known to them.

The Hebrew word for fear is *yare* (pronounced yaw-ray), and it means fearing or reverent (see Strong's Exhaustive Concordance #H3373). Reverence is defined as a feeling of deep respect and awe. The act of worship puts your fear—your reverence and awe of God—into action.

If you are confused by the Bible's use of the word fear and worship in the same verse, you're not alone. It can be hard to understand. What do you imagine you would do if Jesus Christ showed up in your living room or in your church? Maybe you imagine that if Jesus actually revealed himself as a physical presence you would run up to Him and dance around and give Him a hug.

But if you look at what people do when they are confronted with the Angel of the Lord or Jesus you see that they have entirely different reactions. See how John reacts when he sees Jesus as He really is:

> I turned around to see the voice that was speaking to me. And when I turned I saw seven golden lampstands, and among the lampstands was someone "like a son of man," dressed in a robe reaching down to his feet and with a golden sash around his chest. His head and hair were white like wool, as white as snow, and his eyes were like blazing fire. His feet were like bronze glowing in a

furnace, and his voice was like the sound of rushing waters. In his right hand he held seven stars, and out of his mouth came a sharp double-edged sword. His face was like the sun shining in all its brilliance. When I saw him, I fell at his feet as though dead. Then he placed his right hand on me and said: "Do not be afraid. I am the First and the Last (Revelation 1:12-17a).

Whatever you have imagined you would do when you see Jesus, it's more likely that you would do exactly what John did. You would fall at His feet as though dead because you fear Him. It's not that you are terrified of Him in some kind of evil way as if He might strike you or otherwise hurt you. It's that the immensity of His awesomeness is impossible to grasp. The sight of Christ like this would completely overwhelm us. Yet Christ, true to His nature, reaches down and touches us and says, "Don't be afraid."

As we return to Psalm 25:14, we can better understand what David was getting at. We can now understand the use of the word "fear" in this passage as meaning worship with reverence and awe. If we can read the passage using the word "worship" in place of the word "fear," then we can better understand what the writer is getting at. And then we can discover the power of this passage for our lives today.

> The Lord confides in those who fear him; he makes his covenant known to them (Psalm 25:14).

In fact, both the Message version and the Amplified version of the Bible use the word worship in place of the word fear:

> God-friendship is for God-worshipers;

They are the ones he confides in (Psalm 25:14, the Message).

The secret [of the sweet, satisfying companionship] of the Lord have they who fear (revere and worship) Him, and He will show them His covenant and reveal to them its [deep, inner] meaning (Psalm 25:14, Amplified Bible).

The psalmist is saying that as we worship the Lord He begins to confide in us. As I started to ponder what it means to have the Lord confide in us, I thought of what I see when I watch sports sometimes.

A team is having a difficult time in the game. The coach calls a timeout. He motions for one of the players to come over to him. He puts his arm around him, and whispers in his ear. We don't know what he is saying, but we know the coach is giving the player some information about what the other team is doing and how the player can beat them. The timeout is over. The player hits the field or the court. You can see they've changed their strategy, and all of a sudden the game changes. What happened? The coach confided in the player. Because the player had a relationship with the coach built on respect and belief, he made the changes the coach was asking him to make. The player learned something more about the game. When he employed the actions the coach told him to take the player was able to change the outcome of the game.

The promise of Psalm 25:14 is as simple as it sounds. When you worship and fear the Lord, He will respond in the way He says He will, and He will coach you in the ways of His covenant. He will show you what to do when the chips are down and you don't know how to win. In a way, this passage can be thought of like a mathematical equation. If you determine to worship Him, then God will begin to share things with you that He has not been able to trust you with before. He will be able to show you things that you have missed in your walk with Him. The things He shows you will change your life.

Another important thing about worship is that it brings you face to face with your Savior. He wants to spend time with you in fellowship. How do you fellowship with Christ? How do you get to know Him? Most of us have been taught that reading the Bible, praying and reasoning with other believers about the things of God is fellowshipping with Christ, getting to know Him. Reading and praying and talking about God are wonderful ways of deepening our knowledge of God. The dynamic energy of these interactions is fueled by our intellect. God gave us brains to think about Him. He wants us to use our minds in our approach to Him.

But something changes when we worship. Our hearts fuel the dynamic energy of a worship interaction with God. God gave us our hearts to go beyond our intellect in our relationship with Him. It is with our hearts that we truly worship God, even as it is with our hearts that we love our families and friends. It is with our hearts we believe. And it is our belief, or faith, that saves us.

> And without faith it is impossible to please God, because anyone who comes to Him must believe that He exists and that He rewards those who earnestly seek Him (Hebrews 11:6).

If we were to be honest with ourselves, we would admit that the reason we work so hard to understand God intellectually is so that we can have this heartfelt experience with Him. We've seen other believers who have found God as they earnestly sought Him. We want to find Him in the same way. Unfortunately, it is our intellect that ends up guarding our hearts by arguing that

95

we don't have to raise our hands or our voices in worship or make any other display of emotion. The real problem is that whether we raise our hands or don't, whether we shout or don't, we must surrender our hearts and will to God and worship Him with everything we have. One thing is sure: God is not put off by wild worship. David danced before the Lord in his undergarments as the Ark of the Covenant was brought back to Jerusalem. See the difference between God's response and his wife's response to David's worship in 2 Samuel 6. After his wife's critical response to David, the Lord made her barren.

Samuel told Saul that the Lord was going to replace him: "…the Lord has sought out a man after his own heart and appointed him leader of his people" (1 Samuel 13:14). Of course, that man was David. The significant difference between Saul and David is that Saul sought to hear from God through prophets, seers and witches. David sought to hear from God directly and the prophets in his life confirmed what he heard. He was able to hear from God directly because he spent so much time worshipping Him.

As we worship God, we grow in our relationship with Him, and He becomes our Teacher and Coach. As we grow in personal worship, we will find a growing intimacy with Him, we will learn to know Him better. While the style of worship we may employ can vary, there are consistent characteristics that we should learn or consider.

One of the major functions of our worship of God is ascribing worth to Him and submitting our wills to Him. It is easy for most of us to ascribe worth to God. Most Christians would agree that God is worthy of our praise and worship.

It is the act of submitting our will to Him that is difficult. God allows us the choice to submit our hearts and our wills to Him. If we're not choosing to worship Him with everything we have, we'll miss out on this opportunity to learn from Him and become close to Him. At the same time we want to follow Abraham's example. He chose to give up the right to worship God in his own way, his own style, so to speak when he took Isaac to the altar.

We must choose to be willing to strive to worship both corporately (in our churches) and personally. This is an important point. Many of us attend churches with excellent worship programs. We have Christian radio and we can download the latest songs from the Internet. The challenge we face is to decide to personally worship the Lord when we are alone, when it's not Sunday, even if we aren't musicians. We have this challenge because it is so easy to think that if we sing a few songs on Sunday and listen to a good special number by the choir, we have actually worshipped the Lord. Our personal worship of God is what helps us establish a personal connection with God. Our personal worship of God will not only help us develop an intimate relationship with Him, it will bring more depth to our corporate worship experience.

This is where your decision to personally worship God becomes important. In the same way that we said becoming a thankful person is a matter of making a purposeful decision, it is the same with worship. You won't become a thankful person by accident. You won't become a worshipper of God by accident, either.

> "Look! Here I stand at the door and knock. If you hear me calling and open the door, I will come in, and we will share a meal as friends" (Revelation 3:20).

97

It may be hard to believe that we can have intimacy with God. It is a foreign concept to many people. This passage in Revelation gives a clear picture of what we are striving for. We are on the other side of the door from Christ. He knocks on the door because He is seeking us out for fellowship. Think about that for a minute. Imagine one of your closest friends calling you on the telephone and asking to meet you for dinner. You pick a restaurant and a time to meet. When you arrive you greet your friend and dispense with the pleasantries. Then comes the awkward silence. When your dinner arrives, you both make a couple of weak efforts at conversation while you're eating. The next thing you know, the bill comes and dinner is over.

If you had a bona fide chance at a face-to-face dinner with Jesus Christ, would you miss the opportunity to ask Him all of your questions, tell Him your heart's desires, your hopes and dreams for your family? I hope not. Would He miss the chance to ask you lots of questions, tell you His heart's desires and His hopes and dreams for you and your family? According to what we know about Christ from the Word, He is deeply interested in us. I believe that he will listen to us because He cares. And He knows intimacy isn't one-sided.

Here He is. Can you hear Him knocking? Will you open the door to Him? As you begin to purposefully worship Him, He will make Himself known to you. You can have the intimate fellowship He is offering.

If you want to know God … worship God.

When we're confronted with the challenge of personally worshipping God on more than just Sunday morning, we find ourselves with both the problem of **how** to worship and the problem of **when** to worship.

As I mentioned in the previous chapter, when I finally understood the instruction, "If you want to know God, worship God," I didn't know what to do. So, I decided to do what I did know how to do, which was to say, "Praise the Lord!" a lot. It was a couple of months of persisting in personally worshipping God before God met me. Looking back, it didn't seem to take long at all. It can be the same for you. Start worshipping God by doing what you know how to do. The real key is that you make a decision to worship God and pursue it until you understand what the Lord wants from you in worship.

If you went to my church you would know I was there, because you would hear me sing loud and shout loudly to the Lord. Most of the other people in the congregation are somewhat quieter than I am. At first, when I was beginning to receive this revelation about worship, I thought everyone should be loud like me. One time a person sitting in front of me actually asked me to be quiet because I was hurting her ears. It was surprising to me that not everyone seemed to be as excited as I was to worship God. At the same time I was troubled by her response. I spoke with my pastor several times to make sure that I wasn't stepping out of bounds with the church. He assured me each time I talked with him that my style of worship was acceptable. While I do care about other people, and I have mellowed a little over the years, I have determined that no rock is going to cry out praise and worship of God for me. I want to worship him myself.

You may have noticed I haven't suggested that you worship God in any particular way. I struggled with how to talk about this issue for a long time. Finally, I asked the Lord how to teach others to worship Him.

At the time I was involved in a class for new believers. I was a table leader. Our team was getting ready for a weekend retreat. We were gathered for a time of intercession for the weekend and we all prayed, one after the other. When it was the turn for the woman next to me to pray, two things stood out about her prayer. First, she prayed so quietly, I could barely hear her. And she was sitting right next to me. Second, and more importantly, she prayed with intensity, even though she was quiet. She wasn't using volume to make her prayer to God, but she was certainly exerting her heart in it. I couldn't hear her very well, but I could surely feel her prayer.

That's when I realized the answer to this question about *how* to worship God. This woman's prayer was, for me, a great illustration of worship, too. The key in both prayer and worship is to bring Him everything you have. He loves it all. Whether your worship of Him is quiet or loud, still or active, what He wants in your worship is all of your heart. That's why what Hayford says about worship is so important. We have to choose to give our entire self, our entire will over to God.

You may be concerned that you'll look silly or that you don't know how to worship Him. David looked pretty silly worshipping God in his underwear. His wife, Michal, even said so, and it brought a curse on her (see 2 Samuel 6:23). But God is glad to have your worship. He desires your worship. As valuable as He is, He values your worship whatever it sounds like, whatever it looks like. God can manage missed notes and clumsy clapping. But He can't have a full relationship with someone who won't give Him all of his or her heart. He told us to make a joyful noise. Whether or not you sing well or look good while you're doing it, make some noise in worship of the One True Living God. Make this covenant with Him today, right now. It's that important.

As you make a decision to personally worship God and determine that you will surrender your will to Him, you'll have to figure out *when* to worship Him. Establishing a personal worship connection with God requires time and effort. No one learns how to read by going to school one hour a week and then not doing any homework. Neither can you learn to worship by going to church for an hour or so per week and then not do your 'homework.' You will have to spend time personally worshipping God to establish that connection.

Keep in mind that Jesus said His yoke is easy and His burden is light. You do have to make the decision to personally worship God. You do have to find some time to personally worship. Here are a couple of ideas that may help. Worship God in your car on the way to work or to meet with your friends. Worship while you are getting ready for the day. Take a walk in your neighborhood and worship Him. This can be kind of fun, because it feels like you are Enoch walking with God. You can worship while you do chores around the house. There are a lot of things you do during the day that have room for you to worship the Lord.

The primary value of personal worship as a weapon of spiritual war lies in the growth of your relationship with God as your teacher and the development of a more intimate relationship with Him. When you look at David's life, you can see how his relationship with God was developed and strengthened through worship. Because he had such a relationship with God, he heard from God in every situation, whether his need was for defense or offense. If you wait for a battle to begin to build your relationship with God through worship, you will be a step behind. If you've already begun to take the step of personally worshipping God and making an intimate connection with Him, you will be more able to rely on Him for help in a time of trouble.

Make your covenant with God today. Say to Him, "You are my God, and I make a covenant with you that you are my God and I will worship you."

Chapter 9

Worship as Warfare

We've talked about why we should worship: Because we want to know God. We've talked about how to worship: With all of our hearts.

But, how can we see our worship of God as a weapon to use in our battles? What is it about worship that makes it useful in this spiritual war?

Let's say you're facing a battle right now. You may be about to lose everything you hold dear. The circumstances may have brought you to the lowest place you've ever been.

How can you worship? What good is worship when you're already so weak you can hardly look up?

If you've ever been in this kind of circumstance, you can relate to this story about David found in 1 Samuel 30.

David's been on the run from Saul, the king of Israel, for what seems like forever. It was so bad that David stayed in the camp of Israel's enemy—the camp of Achish, the Philistine—for over a year.

As Israel and the Philistines readied for battle, Achish's men began to worry about David turning on them during the fight. They told Achish to send David back to Israel, because they believed he was a spy.

Achish finally agreed with his men and sent David and his men on their way. They returned to their camp to find that the Amalekites had raided the camp and taken the women and children as prisoners. David's men were angry. What was he going to do?

> David was greatly distressed, for the men spoke of stoning him because the souls of them all were bitterly grieved, each man for his sons and daughters. But David encouraged and strengthened himself in the Lord his God (1 Samuel 30:6, Amplified Bible).

"David encouraged and strengthened himself in the Lord." How did he do that? What did he do to encourage himself? What did he do to strengthen himself?

David's heart was troubled at this time. How would you feel if you were in his shoes? He had lost his own family and possessions. That was bad enough. But every one of his men had lost everything, too. And they were mad. We can guess that David was not only afraid and worried, but angry, too.

There were really only two things he could have done to find strength and courage in a situation like this: He remembered what God had done before, and he worshipped God.

It stands to reason that remembering what God had already done for him was a good way for David to find courage and strength. What could David remember? He could remember the lion and the bear that he slew while tending sheep. He could remember his triumphant encounter with Goliath. He could remember how God kept him alive even when the king of Israel was out to kill him.

Remembering these things and saying them out loud and in his heart built up a testimony of who God had been in his life. These testimonies provided a foundation David could build on to strengthen his grip on God's love and power. He was reminding himself that God had already helped him find victory in such great battles. He could then begin to say that if God had helped him before, He would surely help him again. This is the remarkable thing about telling your heart a testimony of God's greatness. As David reminded himself of these triumphs he was fanning the flames of his belief in God, his Victor, in the past, in the present and in the future. This is the purpose of remembering what God has already done. Hearing about God's great victories in the past opened David's heart to begin to believe that God would be victorious again. It will be the same for you.

We can imagine that as David grew stronger through these reminders of God's victories, he began to worship.

He began to declare in worship that God is good, and His loves endures forever (Psalm 100:5). He declared that God was his rock and his salvation (Psalm 18:2). He declared the greatness of God (Psalm 66:3). He worshipped God under the shadow of His wing (Psalm 63:7). David began to grow stronger and stronger by declaring in worship who God had been in his life.

As he continued in worship, David began to find courage and strength in his heart. He began to agree with his own testimony. As he continued in worship, he began to believe that God would help him in this time of trouble, a very present time of trouble (Psalm 46:1).

Worship is a weapon of spiritual warfare precisely because it is a two-way communication between you and the Lord. As you declare who God is in your praise, your heart is listening. God receives your praise and your worship and returns a communication to your heart that says He agrees. He agrees that He is victorious. He agrees that He is triumphant. He agrees that He is your shield, your salvation, your rescuer and deliverer. He agrees that He loves you and he receives your love. As you persist in worship, you find that your heart is less afraid. You find that your heart has become stronger. You begin to believe that you will overcome because the God you worship and adore has already overcome your circumstance for you.

After David strengthened and encouraged himself, he asked God what to do.

> David said to Abiathar the priest, Ahimelech's son, "I pray you, bring me the ephod." And Abiathar brought him the ephod. And David inquired of the Lord, saying, "Shall I pursue this troop? Shall I overtake them?"
>
> The Lord answered him, "Pursue, for you shall surely overtake them and without fail recover all" (1 Samuel 30:7-8).

David found an intimacy with God through worship. Because of his relationship with God, David asked Him a question with an expectation that he would get an answer. He knew God would confide in him.   He knew that God would be his coach.   He didn't beat around the bush. He didn't try to get an answer. He asked God, "Shall I do this? Or that?" The implication of the questions was that he would get an answer. God's answer was immediate. "Pursue…"

The result of David's actions in the midst of this real crisis was that he re-established his personal connection with God. He was able to find courage and strength to face his circumstance. Even more, because he made this choice to worship God in the midst of the worst possible time of his life, he was able to communicate with God and receive a direct answer to his question.

The fact that he chose to re-establish his worship connection with God also led to a full recovery of everything his enemies had taken. As you read the story, you can see that he still had to fight. What would have happened if he hadn't strengthened himself in the Lord? His men were about to stone him to death. He had lost his personal connection with God. He was probably afraid. He was probably angry. If he had been able to talk his men out of stoning him and then took them into battle, he might have lost because he would have taken action out of fear or anger. When he decided to turn to the Lord and worship Him, remembering the great things He had done in the past, David was finally able to re-connect with God. This connection gave him what he needed to overcome fear, anger and circumstance.

David's success in this battle and in many others began with the establishment of a personal worship connection with God. He worshipped God over and over. He said he worshipped God every day every time he had a chance (Psalm 145:2). The worship of God was a part of his life. It became his nature to worship God. This is our goal: To make the worship of our One True Living God a part of our nature.

Who wouldn't want to go to war with the greatest general creating the plan that you know will secure victory? Who wouldn't want to have a coach to help them overcome seemingly insurmountable odds? Who wouldn't want to have dinner with their Savior? God has given us an open invitation to worship Him. He made a way for us to find Him when there seemed to be no way. He wants us to worship Him so that He can develop us, strengthen us and grow us into the people He plans for us to become.

This will happen for you as you commit yourself to developing a personal worship connection with God. Teach your heart how to have an intimate relationship with the One who secured your salvation through Jesus Christ, His Son.

I hope you have already made your covenant with God, vowing that He is your God and that you will worship Him.

It's time now to hold up your side of the covenant. Begin to worship God now.

Here's one way to get started: Say, "Praise the Lord." Say it again: "Praise the Lord!"

Prayer:

Lord, I choose to worship you personally. I want you to teach me, to coach me. Holy Spirit, please teach me how to worship. Lord, I love you. I know that you are God. I know that you made a plan to save me and to give me Your love and peace. I worship You. You are awesome, God. I choose to worship. Help me make my worship acceptable in Your sight, Lord. It is my desire to worship you.

In Jesus Name, Amen.

Chapter 10

Honoring the People in Your Life

In the same way choosing thankfulness is a weapon that helps us get free, choosing to honor the important people in our lives—indeed, all people in our lives—is a weapon that will help us find freedom.

Most of us have had at least one difficult relationship in our lives. It may have been with our parents, other members of our family or our co-workers. There are many books written about how to deal with these difficult relationships. Some of them encourage us to be braver and stronger. Some encourage us to do or say things that ease our troubles. The most important instruction in the Bible comes in the Ten Commandments and speaks directly to our most important relationship: the one we have with our parents. For some, the idea of honoring parents is a painful principle to grasp. It's not that it's hard to understand, but that it can be very difficult to work and walk out.

If you've been rejected, neglected, even abused by your parents, you may realize that the enemy has used this most important relationship to catch you in a trap of hurt and pain. If you are caught in this trap and the enemy has kept you captive from God's plan, then I want to encourage you. There is a way for you to find freedom from the traps the enemy has caught you in.

As I get to know my long-time friends, sometimes I hear them talk about their parents. Along the way I've learned that everyone has different experiences with this most important relationship. Some have grown up having difficult relationships with their parents. Others have grown up with the most rewarding and nurturing relationships with their parents that anyone could ever imagine.

For instance, my wife and another of our good friends love their parents. They were treated well and raised well. They can't remember a time when they didn't feel loved and empowered. On the other hand, I have another friend whose father left his family when he was a little boy. His father was hard and bitter. My friend's older brother was so hurt that he left for Australia when he was young and has never come back. My friend has reconciled with his father a little bit, but it's a tenuous relationship.

My friend Bob was diagnosed with a chronic disease a few years ago. When he told his mother about the disease and what the doctors understand about the genetics of the problem, his mother and his brother rejected him. They couldn't bear to hear that such disease could be related to his family. Over time, the relationship has been healed, but it was painful for all involved for some time.

Steve was beaten terribly by his father. We talked about it years later. At the time, he struggled with bitterness. He finally somewhat reconciled with his father before his father's death, but Steve still struggled with that relationship.

When my grandfather died, I met the funeral director with my father, my aunts and a few other family members. We were all talking about how we remembered Grandpa. We laughed a lot, and it was clear that we all loved him very much.

The funeral director mentioned how nice it was that we spoke of Grandpa the way we did. He said that many times family members expressed anger and bitterness with their parents who had just passed away. Families will have arguments, and children will say awful things about their parents … right there in the funeral home.

It should come as no surprise to us that God has addressed our relationships with our parents. In fact, He is quite clear how we are to treat them. The verses below are among many that cover our relationships with our folks. We'll discuss them more fully as we progress through this chapter.

- Exodus 20:12, "Honor your father and your mother…"
- Ephesians 6:3, "Children, obey your parents in the Lord, for this is right. Honor your father and mother…"
- Colossians 3:20, "Children, obey your parents in everything…"

It's interesting to note that this one command is so important that a beneficial promise is made to those who keep it. Look at the promises and benefits that *will* be fulfilled when you begin to change how you speak and think about your parents:

- Exodus 20:12, "…so that you may live long in the land the Lord your God is giving you."
- Ephesians 6:3, "…that it may go well with you and that you may enjoy long life on earth."
- Colossians 3:20, "…for this pleases the Lord."

I first began to understand these scriptures during an argument with my father. I had been away from home for several years, first joining the military and then attending college away from home. During those years I was far from the Lord. When I was 23, I realized that my lifestyle was catching up to me. I had no money, I was failing my classes and I was unhappy with my direction. At the end of the school year, I was completely broke and rather desperate. I called my father. He came to get me and helped me move home. My plan was to spend the summer at my folks' house and then go back to the college I had been attending.

During the summer I took the chance to re-commit my life to Christ. I then enrolled in the college in my hometown. For most of that first year, I lived with my father. My mother was traveling a lot at the time, so Dad and I had a lot of time to spend together. To say that we had some rough spots would be an understatement. Dad was a great man of God. I was not. We had never communicated well with each other. Now that we were stuck living together, we had a chance to knock off some of the sharp edges.

One day we were bickering about who should have cleaned up the kitchen, He said something I didn't like, and I said, "Yeah? Well, you were a rotten dad!" All of a sudden my father became still. Then he said something so important that it is still shaping my life today. He said, "You know in Ephesians 6:1-3, where it says to honor your parents? It doesn't say to honor them if they are good. It doesn't say don't honor them if they are bad parents. It just says to honor them."

I didn't know it at the time, but I had been caught in a trap. I became afraid of my dad when I was a little boy. He was so big and I was so small that when he spanked me he scared me. As I grew up, I resented him because of that fear. I was angry with him when I was a teenager for most of the reasons teenagers become angry with their parents. Every time I thought of my dad, I decided that he was a bad parent. When he explained this commandment to me the way he did, it caught my attention. I heard what he said and what the Word said, and I made one simple decision: I began to speak well of my dad whenever I could. Then I began to speak well of him when it was difficult.

When I made the decision to honor my father, I didn't get goose bumps, I didn't fall down, I didn't feel a buzz. I don't know exactly what happened in the spiritual realms. But I can tell you that as I continued to work at honoring my father, the Lord completely changed me and released me from the trap I was in.

At first honoring my dad was an effort. But, the more I worked at it, the easier it became. Over the years I found that the honor I had for my dad became affection. I found that I could tell him I loved him and mean it. I loved my Dad. Instead of being difficult to talk to, dad began to initiate conversations. He would ask me my thoughts about the news of the day, and we talked about God. When we talked about things, I knew what he meant and what he felt. I talked to him two or three times a week. We would joke with each other and laugh. He became a great father. The fact that I can say that is a testimony to the power of this principle in spiritual warfare. It's a testimony to the power of honoring the important people in your life.

The decision I made that day to honor my father produced such change in me that it allowed for a great change in my relationship with my dad. I was 45 years old when he died unexpectedly. I had spent more than 20 years honoring him according to the command from the Word. Sometimes honoring him was difficult, but most of the time it was easy. The year before he died, I missed sending him a Father's Day card...again. So, instead of sending a lame card that would be late, I wrote him a letter. I said this in my note to him:

"I love you as my father, but I want you to know that I consider you one of my best friends."

Your choice to honor the important people in your life is powerful for setting you free from the trap of difficult relationships. When you determine to honor your parents, and continue in your efforts, you will find yourself released from the snare of bitterness and resentment.

For those of you who have had great relationships with your parents and for whom this command has been easy, you may still have difficulties with other relationships. Think about the people in your life that the Lord requires you to honor. How well do you get along with your brothers and sisters? What about your boss and co-workers? Let's make an even finer point. How well do you get along with your pastors, the church staff and the people you sit with on Sunday mornings? How about your neighbors and your friends?

As we begin a discussion of how to honor the important people in our lives, it's time to establish an understanding of what we mean by honor and how it relates to love. I see honor as an action. The action of honor simply means to hold a person in respect and to revere or esteem them. Generally speaking, the action that indicates our honor of a person is what we say about them, how we talk about them. In the context of love, honor is a defining characteristic, a part of the definition of love, especially when we are thinking of love as an action.

The Bible is clear in its instruction about how we are to treat the people in our lives. We are to honor them. If they are in authority over us, we are to submit to them as well.

> Submit yourselves for the Lord's sake to every authority instituted among men ... Show proper respect to everyone: Love the brotherhood of believers, fear God, honor the king (1 Peter 2:13, 17).

> "Love the Lord your God with all your heart and with all your soul and with all your mind." This is the first and greatest commandment. And the second is like it: "Love your neighbor as yourself" (Matthew 22:37-39).

It's always easy to obey these scriptures and others like them when we already love the people we work with or live with. Of course, it's much harder to love our neighbors when they don't like us or we don't agree with them. It's even harder to honor and love them when they have hurt us badly.

From the time I left home until I was in my thirties, I couldn't keep a job to save my soul. I lost or left all those jobs because I created an atmosphere around me of bitterness, resentment and pride. I thought I was smarter than my bosses and my co-workers, and I said so ... to everyone who would listen. I was surprised when the people I talked to told others what I said. I was easily offended and became offensive to others because of it. When someone asked me to do something I thought was beneath me, I refused to do it. I was great at rationalizing my actions and terrible at understanding the responses of others when I was being so offensive. I created this terrible atmosphere around me by what I said and thought.

How you talk and think about the people in your life actually creates a great deal of your experience with them and with the rest of your world.

Jesus spoke about the impact to our own lives because of what we say and think. He said we can know what kind of world we are creating for ourselves just by listening to our thoughts and speech. On one of these occasions, the Pharisees were pressuring Jesus about his lack of adherence to Jewish tradition because the disciples weren't washing their hands before they ate. In His typical fashion, Jesus was ready for their pressure and responded with a sharp rebuke of his own. He accused them of breaking the fifth commandment (Exodus 20:12) to honor their parents. He called the Pharisees hypocrites and judged them for creating a tradition that allowed children to bypass the commandment by giving money to the church instead of using it to support their aging parents. It's one thing not to wash your hands, He was saying, it's another to dishonor your parents (by not taking care of them). He followed His judgment with this:

> Jesus called the crowd to him and said, "Listen and understand. What goes into a man's mouth does not make him 'unclean,' but what comes out of his mouth, that is what makes him 'unclean' " (Matthew 15:10-11).

A little bit later Jesus explained to the disciples what He meant. He told them that unwashed hands don't make a person unclean (with regard to the Law). Instead, what a person says makes him unclean. With regard to speaking about the people in your life, what you say about your parents and others in your life will reveal whether you have a clean heart.

In Luke we hear Jesus say something similar:

> "No good tree bears bad fruit, nor does a bad tree bear good fruit. Each tree is recognized by its own fruit. People do not pick figs from thornbushes, or

116

grapes from briers. The good man brings good things out of the good stored up in his heart, and the evil man brings evil things out of the evil stored up in his heart. For out of the overflow of his heart his mouth speaks (Luke 6:43-45).

Jesus clearly shows us what we need to change. We need to change what is in our hearts towards the people who have hurt us or offended us. Failure to change what is in our hearts will leave us forever caught in the enemy's trap. The problem is that it is sometimes hard to tell what is in our hearts, let alone how it got there.

We are creatures of thought. All of us have many thoughts occurring at the same time. Our brains are monitoring many things while we go about our day. For example, right now you may be at a coffee shop having a white mocha while you're reading this book. As you're waiting you notice that it's a little bit cool in the coffee shop. At the same time you are hearing a conversation at the table next to you and wondering how your kids are doing in school and with their friends. Some thoughts stir us to action and others are discarded. You notice it's cold in the coffee shop, but not cold enough to move or put a sweater on. You decide that when you get home you'll ask one of your children how her studies and grades are coming along.

Feelings are wrapped up in all of these thoughts. Our emotions are involved in our decisions and consequently our choices for action or inaction. When it comes to difficult relationships, we will have a thought, often accompanied by a feeling, followed by a decision and then an action. You may observe that a feeling precedes a thought, and that can also be true. The net effect of all of this is what leads us to where we are in the relationship.

In other words, the decisions we make about our thoughts and feelings when we're in a difficult relationship will either lead us into a trap or out of a trap. The great thing about this chain of events is that we can remove ourselves from a trap if we have been caught in one regardless of how long we have been there. Getting out of a trap is a matter of changing the decisions we have made in the relationship and teaching our heart what we want it to say.

This is how you can tell if you are caught in a trap: Listen. Listen to what you are saying to yourself and others about the people in your life. This will reveal what is in your heart. Whether you talk about the people who have offended you frequently or rarely, you may be stuck in the trap. By the way, it doesn't matter if you never talk to another person about your anger and bitterness—it matters what you say when you are by yourself, too. It's important to hear what you're saying to yourself and others about these relationships.

I know that many of you have good reason to be angry and bitter. Remember what's been said about this. What happened to you in these difficult relationships may not be your fault. But you are responsible for the decisions you've made and the things you've said to yourself and to others since the experience happened.

When you listen to yourself, it's kind of like taking your own temperature. Every once in a while I catch myself rehearsing being angry. Sometimes, it's completely ridiculous. I'll have the radio on and hear a news story or other commentary. I start to think about the story and then begin to rehearse what I would say if I were the victim in the story. I'll be giving the offender a real talking to. And then I realize I'm chewing out someone in a news story that has nothing to do with my life. They haven't hurt me, they don't even know me and I'm yelling at them in my imagination. It dawns on me that rehearsing how to be angry with someone, anyone, is a bad idea. I don't want to do that. Do you? Do you want the defining characteristic of your life to be anger or resentment or bitterness? What about depression and withdrawal? You want to be free from this kind of entanglement. You want to avoid the traps and the snares the enemy has set for you. So, listen to yourself and take your own temperature on a regular basis.

I've worked through this recently. I heard myself talking about an important relationship in my life and I heard anger and bitterness. As soon as I heard it, I knew I would have to go to the Lord and work things out. The person I'm having difficulty with doesn't know I'm struggling. I don't need to let them know. I do have to get my heart right before the Lord.

Once we recognize that we are caught in the trap of dishonoring our parents and other people in our lives, we have to tell the truth about it. We have to repent of what we think and say about them. They treated us poorly. They should have done better. There's no question about it. But, it doesn't matter what they did or didn't do. We have to take responsibility for the decisions we've made about our own lives because of these relationships. As we take responsibility for our selves and take the problem to the Cross, we are forgiven.

The Lord's standard is different than ours. His plan is better than ours. Sometimes it's necessary for us to do some work to remove those things that are keeping us from His perfect plan.   When you listen to yourself you can know your own condition.

I mentioned earlier that I know a man who was beaten terribly by his father. I've known this man since I was 10 years old. He is one of the sweetest, most joyful men you'll ever meet, if you have the privilege. I didn't know anything about his youth until just a couple of years ago. Steve (not his real name) had moved back to the family farm to take care of his father and mother. I visited him at the farm one day and we began to talk about his father who had recently passed away. In fact, we talked about both our fathers. I told him the story of the argument I had with my father, the decisions I made and the result so many years later.

Steve told me more me about his father. He described how his father had beaten him, and he told me that he didn't know how to honor him. I agreed that it would be hard. I reminded him of how I had done it and what I had learned through the process. I suggested that he ask the Holy Spirit to teach him what to say. Even though his father had passed away, Steve could still honor him. He agreed to do this.

Steve and I talked a few weeks after this. He shared with me what the Holy Spirit had shown him. He was able to honor his father by saying that he learned two good things from him. He said his father taught him how to obey and how to tell the truth.

Maybe it doesn't seem like much to be able to say something so simple, so nice about a man who had beaten his son so severely. But in saying it, agreeing with it and accepting it, Steve began to teach his heart. As he taught his heart, and changed his decisions about this relationship, he began to feel a release from the trap he was in.

In the Amplified version of Luke 6:45, we see the passage translated this way:

> The upright (honorable, intrinsically good) man out of the good treasure [stored] in his heart produces

what is upright (honorable and intrinsically good), and the evil man out of the evil storehouse brings forth that which is depraved (wicked and intrinsically evil); for out of the **abundance** (overflow) of the heart his mouth speaks. (emphasis mine) Luke 6:45.

This is how we know that the abundance of Steve's heart changed. He found freedom when he changed the decisions he made in his heart about his father. When he did this, he was able to change what he said to himself about his father. As he began to teach his heart, he began to change his "self talk." He changed how he spoke with others about his father. He found he was finally able to say, "I loved my dad. He taught me how to be obedient and how to tell the truth." As he took these steps, Steve began to find the freedom from being angry and bitter with his father. Freedom from anger and bitterness helped him know the true love of God in a deeper and more meaningful way.

Here's the easiest way to know what kind of world we are creating for ourselves. Referring back to the passage in Luke 6:45, "…For out of the overflow of his heart his mouth speaks," you can learn about your heart by listening to what you say when you are under stress. What do you say, what do you feel when you are upset with the person you are thinking of? This is what is in the abundance of your heart.

As a young man I blamed my parents for my problems. I spoke about them from the abundance of my heart. I was angry and bitter and resentful of them. Whenever I experienced stress of some kind, I would blame them. I would burn in anger toward them. Yet I called them every Saturday morning without fail. I talked to them about the events of the week and when I hung up I told them I loved them. This is important for you to understand. I did love my parents. But, I was also very angry with them. That anger impacted every area of my life.

It wasn't until I began to change my decisions about them that things began to change for me. I had to listen to what I said to myself and to others about my parents. I had to correct what I said. Some of the decisions were easy to change. Others were harder. Ultimately, I was rewarded for the changes. I had an increasingly better relationship with my parents and with other people in my life.

It's your choice to establish this pattern of listening to yourself and recognizing when you are saying things that aren't honoring the important people in your life. When you recognize that you are about to fall into this trap, choose to tell the truth, then repent and change what you are saying about the people and the circumstance.

I was on a social networking site a while ago, and someone wrote this question about their day: "Will things get better if I say, 'I love my job, I love my job, I love my job?'" The answer to the question is this: If you change the decisions you make about your job, things will get better for you. It's not that saying "I love my job" that makes it better, but saying, "I *choose* to love my job" will. We aren't casting magic spells. It's making a decision again and again to love your job, even when it's not lovable, that makes the change within you.

In the same way, it's not saying "I honor this person" that makes honoring them easier. It's making a decision again and again to honor them, even when they don't deserve honor, that makes the change in you.

The people in our lives that we are commanded to honor may not be good people. They may not be nice to you.

122

We can't control who they are or how they act. But we can control our thoughts and our speech. The principle is simple, but sometimes walking it out in our lives is difficult. That's where your choice to take up the battle comes in. When you feel the temptation to complain about someone, that is when the fight is on. It's so easy to surrender to the temptation to complain. The more you complain, the more angry and bitter you become. If you can recognize the battle and forcefully decide against the complaint, you will be able to overcome the circumstance. As you work toward overcoming the circumstance, you will be better able to hear the Lord instructing you about how to handle it, pray for it and have victory over it. At the least, you will take another step toward a more mature Christian walk.

I find frequently that people aren't quite sure how to pray about situations like this. It can be difficult to know what to say to the Lord if you haven't talked to Him about this kind of trial before. Sometimes people have struggled with important relationships for years, even decades. Whether it's been a long struggle or something that happened today, the basic process is the same.

Here's an example of a prayer that you might say when you find yourself in this kind of fight.

> Father,
> I come before you now, and I want to tell you about the circumstance I'm in. I know you already know about it. But I bring it to you this way to ask You to help me. My (boss, husband, pastor, sister or whoever) did/said this:_____ to/about me. It really hurt. It hurt enough that I am angry about it.

If this has been a long battle, you may want to express a little bit more about what you feel and how this struggle has impacted you. For example:

Father,
I've been so angry and bitter enough about this circumstance that I have made many bad decisions because of it. My decisions have caused me to lose my job (or marriage or family). I have caused other people a great deal of pain because of my decisions about this circumstance.

Lord, I repent of my decisions about this circumstance and about the people involved. I've been wrong and I'm sorry. Please forgive me and cleanse me from all unrighteousness, as Your Word says (I John 1:9).

I know I can't control what others do. But I can control what I do. I choose to forgive (person's name) for doing/saying this to me. I want You to be free to work in my life.

I forgive (person's name). I choose to give this circumstance to you so that I can be free from it. I repent of all the decisions I have already made about this circumstance.

Holy Spirit, I ask you to teach me how to work through this circumstance. I don't know what to say when I think about this it, but I know that You do. Thank you for teaching me how to have victory today.

In Jesus Name, Amen

Chapter 11

Forgiving the People in Your Life

Once upon a time there were two sisters. They lived in a nice house in a little town in the Midwest of the United States. Carol was an only child until, at 12 years old, she found herself with a brand-new baby sister. It was difficult for Carol when Alice was born, since she had been the only child for so long. Alice, for her part, only knew that sometimes Carol was mean to her. Carol went off to college and then married John and they moved to another midwestern town, where John became a traveling salesman. Sometime later of course, Alice also went off to college. Then she married Ralph. Alice and Ralph moved to a different midwestern town, where Ralph became an attorney.

In the early years of their marriage, Alice and Ralph would see Carol and John at the lake home of the girls' parents. For the most part, they seemed to get along, and yet there was always an undercurrent of tension between them. Alice was sometimes quite mean to Carol's daughters, so much so that Ralph occasionally stepped in to protect them. As life continued for the sisters, they grew further apart and eventually they became quite angry with each other. The amount of time they spent together dwindled to once every few years, when situations demanded that they had to be together. Then their mother passed away, their father having passed several years before. So came the straw that broke the camel's back

As they began to go through their mother's things, there was a great offense. Carol and John said Alice and Ralph were not raising their children very well. This comment was received poorly. The relationship became even more difficult and the next thing anyone knew, they were no longer on speaking terms.

Their story is much the same as many other families' stories, except for one thing. Years before her mother passed, Alice became a believer. So did Ralph. In fact, Ralph led a Bible study in their hometown that was instrumental in bringing the baptism of the Holy Spirit to many college students. Some of those who knew him well considered him to be a prophet due to the manner of his ministry and his teaching ability.

In the context of their well-founded and devout relationship with the Lord, it seems as though they should have been able to work through the trials of this relationship with Carol and John. But, indeed, whenever the topic of this relationship was brought up to either Alice or Ralph, it was quickly dismissed as something that no one else could understand.

At the time of the great offense, Alice and Ralph were at their own crossroad. Alice had returned to college. Ralph left one job to begin a new law practice in a nearby town. You wouldn't have known it at the time, but the impact of harboring the offense, and the bitterness and unforgiveness that came with it, had a lasting impact on their lives.

Some people thought that Ralph should pursue a broader ministry, with Alice supporting him while growing into her own ministry. Instead, it seemed as though no opportunity would ever come. Alice became a high school teacher, a gifted one at that, and quite well thought of by her students. Ralph, however, seemed to have nothing but struggles with his law practice, never seeming to be able to earn much profit from his labor. Eventually, his ministry all but disappeared.

Both Alice and Ralph died much too young and may well have missed out on the great plans the Lord had for them. It's clear why this happened. When they became offended and determined to hold on to the offense instead of letting it go, it became an anchor to them. It kept them from progressing in their relationship with the Lord.

This story illustrates the difficulties we face in our Christian walk when we fail to forgive those who have offended us. We must understand this in the context of honoring the important people in our lives because these are the people who tend to hurt us the most. As we see in the story above, even experienced, mature Christians struggle with this problem, and their failure to overcome traps them in a prison of twisted perspective and limited or terminated opportunity.

If we have any hope of finding the life that Christ died for us to have, a life full of love and grace beyond our imagination, we have to choose to overcome the kinds of difficulties that arise simply from having relationships with people. We have to choose to leave this place of bitterness. We have to choose to break our hardness of heart to find the healing and restoration that we have through Christ.

Many times, when we have trouble honoring our parents, our husbands and wives, our bosses and co-workers, our brothers and sisters, or even our pastors, it is because we have become offended.

Once we have become offended, we are faced with the temptation to hold on to the offense. Giving in to this temptation will lead us on a path to the trap the enemy has set for us. The path to freedom follows these two steps:

1) We have to recognize the offense.

2) We have to fight to be free of the offense.

Our path to freedom is found in forgiveness. As hard as it is, forgiveness is ultimately one of the most important acts you can commit as a believer, and therefore it is one of our most important weapons. And unforgiveness is one of the enemy's most important weapons he uses against us.

It is my observation that most people misunderstand the concept of forgiveness. I hear many people say that you should forgive and forget. They say that they take this to mean forgive until you forget. Here's what's interesting about this idea. Psychological studies have been done with survivors of the Holocaust. The purpose of the study was to evaluate whether the survivors had suffered so much trauma that they blocked out or forgot what happened to them. The findings were that the survivors remembered in great detail the atrocities that they witnessed and suffered. If they were to work through all of the trauma of their experience of the Holocaust and forgive their torturers, it is unlikely they would forget what happened to them. It's the same for us. As we work through the offenses and trauma we have experienced, we are unlikely to forget those things.

However, it is possible to forgive until the offense doesn't matter. The question is how do we forgive until we've attained this victory?

To frame the question better, let's state it this way: How can we forgive until we have been delivered from the bondage that unforgiveness and bitterness entangles us in?

Remember we have said that the experiences and events we have lived through may not be our fault. But, the decisions we have made as a result of them have been and continue to be our responsibility.

Telling the truth, accepting responsibility for our actions and repenting of them are important steps in finding deliverance from our current circumstance. When we take these steps, we address things in our lives that are there as a result of holding on to the offense.

When we are offended to the extent that we need to forgive a person or persons, we need to change our strategy. Our focus has been to be freed from sin: anger, worry, fear, etc. Now our focus is to be freed from bondage, from being tied to an event or experience in which we received an offense.

Unforgiveness and bitterness are sometimes rooted in events that are not our fault. Other times our own actions have opened the door in such a way that we become offended. Generally, we have been injured in some way through the actions or words of another person. We find ourselves in need of deliverance because we have persisted in choosing to remain hurt and in pain. Remaining in this state of hurt creates a world around us that continues to cause us pain. Our ties to this hurt have become so strong that we are in bondage to the event or experience. We are also in bondage to the pain of the event. Our objective in choosing to persist in forgiveness is to cut the ties to this event or experience.

One day a ship set its sails for a far away destination. The journey would take a very long time. The captain addressed the passengers and crew as soon as their journey was under way. Shore leave was planned for several ports of call and some of the harbors were hard to get into. In addition, the captain said a journey of this length was bound to encounter one or two storms along the way.

Eventually, as the captain predicted, the ship encountered a storm and had to put down its anchor in the cove of a small island. The next morning the ship prepared for the next leg of the journey. The first mate went to pull up the anchor, and he couldn't budge it. The anchor was stuck fast. He called another mate for help, but the two of them couldn't move it. None of their efforts seemed to have the intended effect. Soon the crew and some of the passengers began to argue, asking how this could have happened and whose fault it was. Now all their efforts seemed to be directed at laying blame and finding fault. And the ship was still stuck by its anchor.

Finally, the captain asked what the problem was. The first mate explained to him that the anchor was stuck. The crowd began to rise in a chorus of shouts and finger pointing. The captain quieted the crowd and thought for a minute. Then he called the first mate to him and whispered in his ear. The first mate looked at the captain and shook his head. He said, "This anchor is too important to leave behind. I can't see how we can leave without it." He became angry and started shouting at the captain, "You don't know what I had to endure to get this anchor! There is nothing more important to us than this anchor. We can't leave without it!"

The captain was silent for a minute, then turned to go back to the bridge. After a few minutes the crew and passengers noticed the captain rummaging for something. Finally, it appeared he found what he was looking for. He returned to them carrying an armload of things.

He faced the first mate and the rest of the crowd. He pulled out the first items he brought with him, the maps and charts used to plan their journey. As he talked about the final destination, about its beauty and the work to be accomplished when they arrived, the crowd became quiet. They began to look around to see that where they were wasn't quite as wonderful as they thought it was. They had become so involved with the anchor that they hadn't had a chance to survey their surroundings.

The captain stepped closer and drew out the second item he had brought from the bridge. The crowd gasped. They saw that the captain had a knife in his hand. He called the first mate back to him and gave him the knife. He said, "I know how important this anchor is. The problem is that it's doing its job so well that we can't get underway until we are free from it. It's your job to cut the lines that are holding us to the anchor." The first mate looked at the captain in silence. You could see that he was thinking long and hard about what the captain said.

"It's a difficult choice you give me, Captain. I know what I want to do, but it's hard for me to leave the anchor behind."

"I understand. It's your choice. We can remain here, or we can cut the line and find out what the rest of the journey has in store. Just remember this: Staying here doesn't guarantee safety or satisfaction."

The first mate didn't move for a minute. Then he nodded his head and turned toward the anchor lines. He had the knife in his hand, and when he reached the lines he began to cut. There were many lines. Some of them were easy to cut, and some were more difficult. He was nearly through the task when he stopped. He took a breath and said, "This one is hard to cut." One of the passengers stepped up to offer his knife. The first mate took it and went back to work. He worked and he worked. He had to take another break because the work was so hard.

After one last great effort from the first mate, they were finally free of the anchor. Everyone could feel the ship lurch, almost as if it had been straining at the lines for some time. The captain commanded, "Let's get under way!" The hands on deck and below deck went to their stations and worked furiously to leave the lagoon. In no time at all everyone on board could feel the sweet ocean breeze on their faces. The sun was shining, and they were once again en route according to the plans that were made before they started out.

Our lives are like the first mate's life and the anchor. The anchor of unforgiveness and bitterness serves to hold us back. It weighs so much, but we have become accustomed to carrying it around. Some of us have been anchored in the same place for so long that we can't imagine life without the anchor and the surroundings we are tied to because of it.

After cutting a few of the lines, forgiving some of the offenses, but not all of them, we might begin to think we are free. We'll just start to feel like we are on the way out of the cove and then our anchor will stop us again and we'll end up right back where we started.

We want to be free. We want restoration in our lives. We want to grow and move on to God's plan for our lives. The only way we can find these things in God is to cut the ties to these offenses by forgiving the ones we have been blaming for our troubles.

If we need deliverance from these events and experiences, then where is it?

Deliverance always starts with truth. Jesus said: "You shall know the truth and the truth shall set you free" (John 8:32). And the truth is that we need to forgive those who have offended us, regardless of the offense.

As we hear the Word of God and apply it to our lives we begin to participate in the battle. The Holy Spirit is leading us to do one thing and the enemy of our souls is leading us to do something else. Sometimes a literal war starts and we can feel it in our souls.

If we fail to forgive, we are following the lead of Satan. The Holy Spirit wants to lead us to freedom. The enemy of our souls wants us to stay in the trap. Satan wants us to stay exactly where we are when we walk in unforgiveness. While we're in this trap, he is free to destroy our lives and steal what God has planned for us.

Look around. Are you where you think you should be? Are you fulfilling God's plan for your life? What's the truth about your situation? Are you out of order with God's word in this area? Then you need to know what steps you should take. It's worth the fight to take on the battle that it takes to obtain freedom.

You'll remember I told you about my friend Steve who had worked so hard to find a way to honor his father. I spoke with him again after he told me of his efforts to honor his father. There was a new development in his story. One Sunday he went to the little country church he attends. The pastor was giving a sermon about the Ten Commandments. Steve, a former pastor, was sitting back, thinking that there wouldn't be too much in this sermon for him. Then the pastor began to talk about the fifth commandment. "Honor your father and mother so that you may live long in the land the Lord your God has given you" (Exodus 20:12). All of a sudden he started paying attention to what the pastor was saying. As he was listening, he realized there was one more thing he had left to do. Steve realized that he still needed to forgive his father. He said, "I forgive you, Dad. I forgive you." When he said this, Steve said he saw a picture of his dad running around in heaven, shouting, "He forgave me. My son forgave me!" Steve believes, and I do, too, that he found freedom when he forgave his father.

In the Word, Jesus concludes His teaching on the Lord's Prayer with these thoughts:

> For if you forgive men when they sin against you, your heavenly Father will also forgive you. But if you do not forgive men their sins, your Father will not forgive your sins …. I will give you the keys of the kingdom of heaven; whatever you bind on earth will be bound in heaven, and whatever you loose on earth will be loosed in heaven (Matthew 6:14-15, 19).

It is clear that the Lord places a great value on our acts of forgiveness when others have hurt us. The impact of forgiving or not is underscored when we hear what Christ says about the spiritual or heavenly consequence of forgiveness. The primary vehicle, or exercise of this binding and loosing, is forgiveness. When we forgive others, we loose heaven to operate for us. When we remain in unforgiveness, we bind heaven from operating for us.

One more time Jesus confirms this principle in Matthew 18:18
> "I tell you the truth, whatever you bind on earth will be bound in heaven, and whatever you loose on earth will be loosed in heaven.

In Jesus' parable of the wicked servant (Matthew 18:21-35), Christ reinforces the idea that God hates unforgiveness. The point of the story is clear. We have been forgiven so much that it is unacceptable to God that we should have unforgiveness against our brothers or hold anything against them. Unforgiveness is incompatible with our faith in Christ. Since the basis of our faith is Christ's love, mercy and grace, it is incompatible with our faith that we should have any other attitude for the people around us.

When you hold on to unforgiveness, it becomes like the anchor in the story of the ship. When you have held onto it for a long time, the lines attached to it are many and they may be quite strong.

If you were able to see the lines we're talking about you would probably see that cutting through them is a job that will take a lot of work. Cutting through those lines may be difficult. Over and over again we will have to take the knife to the lines. We'll have to saw and cut through them until we are completely free.

If you have an anchor like this in your life you can approach the job of cutting those lines by following these steps.

The first step in cutting your lines is to thank God in your situation. You may not be able to thank God *for* the situation, but you can thank Him *in* your situation.

If I get a flat tire during rush hour on a busy freeway I won't be giving thanks for the flat tire. But, I will be thankful that God is protecting me while I am changing the tire. In the same way, when you are in a circumstance in which you are feeling the pain of an injury to your heart, you must begin to give thanks in your situation. It is unlikely that you can genuinely give thanks that someone has caused you pain, but you must find a way to be thankful in your circumstance. For example, you can start by thanking God that He has not forsaken you, He has not left you and that His plan for you is not going to be destroyed because of what someone else has done to you. Ask the Lord to teach you how to be thankful in the circumstance. He will answer your prayer.

The second step is to bless the person or people whom you have had difficulty with. And pray for their good.

I was having a difficult time getting along with someone, and I was trying to pray about the situation. As I prayed I could hear myself imposing my will into the life of the other person. I really wanted God to teach him a lesson, and so I was about to pray, "Dear Lord, please bring my friend to his senses and help him understand what he is so wrong about." It struck me as I was about to make this prayer that instead, I should trust God to work with the other person just as he was working with me. I changed my prayer to "Dear Lord, I pray for good for this person. I trust you to know what good is for him, so I place my trust in you to work for his good, just like you are doing for me."

The third step requires that you do the work it takes to forgive the people who have offended you. Press into the Lord for help with this job. The act of forgiving can be like a battle sometimes. Take a look at Matthew 18:22. Peter just asked, "How many times should I forgive?" And Jesus said "Seventy times seven." That's a lot of forgiving for the same person and the same offense.

I hired a friend to do some work for me. The job seemed to take forever. Finally, he said he would be at my house on a certain day to complete the work. I took a day off from my job so I could help. The time he said he would arrive came and went. He was already about an hour late when I called him only to find out that he was at the airport on his way to Mexico for a vacation. Well, I was pretty steamed about that. After all, my wife wanted the job done, I wanted the job done and I was paying him to do the job. I was beginning to make a list of all the reasons I should be angry and it was working—I was getting more and more angry. But all the time my anger was growing, I could hear my heart and the Holy Spirit reminding me that this guy was my friend and that he needed Jesus. I knew I would have to forgive him or I would say something mean and hurt his feelings.

I began to say out loud that I forgave him. I was happy with myself that I was so wise to do so. About a minute later I was still thinking about the situation, and I began to get mad all over again. I couldn't believe it! So, I forgave him again. And then I got mad again, so I forgave him again. Over and over. It took a couple of days to work through the situation so that I was free from being angry. I never brought the story up to him. I didn't need to. I had forgiven him. But it was a lot of work on my part. I did all that work to forgive someone because they took too long to install a countertop. What if it had been something really important, something really damaging? Then how much work would it have been? How hard would I have to fight to be free from unforgiveness?

It's important to judge yourself to evaluate whether you have actually forgiven or not. An easy way to evaluate your progress in forgiveness is to listen to yourself. Hear what you really say about the person and the situation when it comes up in general conversation. If you're doing well so far, then go to the next level. What happens when the pressure is on and the chips are down? Then what do you say? Who are you blaming? What did they do?

I had an occasion to listen to a couple talk about the difficulties they were facing because of health problems and unemployment. As the wife began to tell her story, I could hear the frustration she felt. I could also hear the unforgiveness and bitterness she was harboring in her heart about being fired from her job. I listened to her tell her story for about half an hour. I asked her a few questions and listened to her answers. Then I said to her that it sounded like she needed to forgive the person who fired her. I was amazed by her response. She told me that she had already forgiven the key person in this situation. Then she said that she felt like I was scolding her. I apologized to her and explained that I intended no more harm to her. I left this experience feeling sad for the couple. I had nothing more to offer them, and it seemed as though she would remain bitter and unhappy for a very long time.

As you work through this evaluation of your circumstance, you may start with the belief that you have completed the work of forgiving. Upon a closer look, though, you may find sticking points, places where your work of forgiveness is incomplete. Be encouraged. You can't forgive someone too much, but you can *not* forgive them enough, leaving the work incomplete. This is where you work through the steps we have outlined. Give thanks, honor and forgive until you know the work of forgiveness is complete. Ask the Holy Spirit to lead you and teach you through the work if you need help. He will be right by your side, ready to coach you as you cut the ties to these anchors that have held you back.

There are at least two reasons to forgive those who have hurt us. First, we forgive others because we have been forgiven so much. Our Father in heaven spent everything He had to provide us with forgiveness. It is our command to forgive others.

When we forgive in obedience to the Word, we find the second reason for making the effort to forgive: freedom. As we obey the command to forgive and then honor the people in our lives, we find freedom. This is what Jesus meant when He said that what we loose on earth is loosed in heaven. When we forgive others, we are loosing, untying and cutting the lines that have held us under oppression and kept us from the deeper walk with God that we have sought.

Chapter 12

Choices

I think one of the best David versus Goliath movies is "Hoosiers." A down on his luck, high-caliber college basketball coach is finally offered a job to coach a tiny high school in Indiana. There are a couple of talented kids on the team, but overall they are a very average team.

On the first day of practice, the coach talks to the players about his philosophy and how they are going to win games. The players take to the floor and begin to practice. It's clear after only a few minutes that none of the players understand the simplest aspects of the game. Nor can they perform them to any high level. They have trouble dribbling and passing, and most of them have trouble making baskets.

The coach interrupts the practice and begins to set up drills to improve the player's skills at the most basic parts of the game. The players are unhappy. They thought they knew how to play basketball. They thought they didn't need a coach. They thought they could win.

This leads to quite a lot of turmoil for the team. One player quits. Another is kicked off the team. The coach works with the players that are left and brings in an assistant to help with practices. This is an unpopular move since the assistant was known as the town drunk. Everywhere the coach turns there's turmoil. Yet he continues to drill his players on the basics of the game.

Over and over they practice dribbling and handling the ball. Over and over they practice passing and making plays instead of shots. Over and over they work on their free throws.

By the middle of the season, both the team and the town are beginning to see significant improvement. The coach continues to work on the disciplines of the game. By the end of the season, the team overcomes everything and makes it through the state tournament to the championship game. It's the little school against the big school. It's an intimidating challenge. At the end, the team with the best play at the basics wins the game. The tiniest school prevails over the greatest giant.

It's a great story. But it only became a great story because the players chose to do what the coach asked of them. They chose to dribble and pass over and over again until it became so natural to them that they could do it in their sleep.

The story of this little team isn't much different than yours and mine. It's exciting and wonderful to concentrate on the big things in our walk with God. But these big, exciting, wonderful things aren't what help us through the trials and the tribulations.

It's the so-called little things that are truly important in our walk. When we practice the little things and become good at them, we will find real freedom to become the mature Christians we've always wanted to be.

You can go to conference after conference and special speaker after special speaker to try to hear from God and find deliverance from your circumstances. Some of you will find that deliverance. That makes for a great story and will certainly bring glory to God. Even so, to live the life that Christ promised, you'll need to continue to choose. You will have to choose to overcome your circumstance through remaining thankful, continuing in personal worship and honoring the people in your life.

It's your choice. To be more accurate, it's your choices. Over and over again, you are being lured into the traps of ungratefulness, isolation from God, and anger and bitterness with the people in your life. You choose thankfulness or ungratefulness. You choose to personally worship God or become isolated from Him. You choose pain and bitterness or forgiveness and freedom.

I urge you to choose to become a thankful person.

I encourage you to establish a personal worship connection with God.

I ask you to find it in your heart to choose to honor and forgive the people in your life who have hurt and offended you.

I know the principles we've talked about are simple. Please don't dismiss them because they are so simple. Practice, practice, practice. Choose these things over and over again, and I know they will help you overcome your circumstances.

Made in the USA
San Bernardino, CA
16 March 2014